The Devil's Will

Anthony C. S. Flanigan

CONTENTS

THIS IS WAR

"Take their weapons away!" my teacher yelled as we would side step a straight right. I would strike the outside of their right elbow with my left palm, simultaneously ridge handing the inside of the forearm with my right hand. This would successfully dismember the right arm. I practiced this move countless times, hoping to never need it. To do this kind of damage to another human seemed so harsh. But then again, they are trying to kill me in this scenario. I suppose when you put it that way, repeat the drill. Side step their strike, palm to elbow, ridge hand to forearm, break the arm, take that weapon away so they never use it against me again. I don't wanna die when the enemy attacks. I want to live and I want to protect myself.

This tactic of self-defense is far from foreign. There are no rules in love and war. If I want to prevail against my enemy, I must take his weapons away.

Now you might read this and think, this is what we are going to do, we are going to pop the Devil's right arm out of socket so we don't get beat up. Not fully my point. My point is, that we are not fighting from the defensive. It's the Devil himself who has been assaulted by Jesus, stripped of all authority; and he is the one trying to disarm and dismember Gods church. The Enemy is attempting to side step our assault and to break the strength of our right arm. The enemy wants us on our defense, and he can only do that after successfully taking away our weapons. The crazy thing, is that snake with his crushed head, still has a mocking little mouth. And out of his crushed face, the snake, our enemy, the Devil himself whispers lies that sound like the soundest doctrine so that we might repeat the lie and tear down the truth. He is getting us to fight for him. This is the Devil's will.

The Devil's will flows from the mind of one of the highest trained war-strategists to ever exist – Lucifer, the fallen archangel. It's so important to realize Lucifer has a sealed fate, cast out of heaven and dreadfully waiting judgment in the lake of eternal fire. Lucifer was the highest-ranking kind of angel, archangel. He led the angels in both worship and battle. The blue angel, Michael, the messenger and archangel of God battled Lucifer and 1/3 of heavens angels were cast out of heaven and now Lucifer's

main objective is to lead the whole world astray.
Revelation 12:7-9 *Then war broke out in heaven. Michael and his angels fought against the dragon, and the dragon and his angels fought back. 8 But he was not strong enough, and they lost their place in heaven. 9 The great dragon was hurled down—that ancient serpent called the Devil, or Satan, who leads the whole world astray. He was hurled to the earth, and his angels with him.*

2 Corinthians 4:4 *The god of this age has blinded the minds of unbelievers, so that they cannot see the light of the gospel that displays the glory of Christ, who is the image of God.*

Lucifer, the Devil, the lower case 'god' of this age, is trained well in warfare strategy. He only has one avenue of attack, his voice, his lies. The Devil knows where to sow lies to reap the most deception and lead the world astray. Do you know where the greatest strategist sows his greatest lies? In the pulpits. Well meaning pastors have been filled with lies from the Devil himself.

2 Corinthians 11:12-15 *But I will keep on doing what I am doing, in order to undercut those who want an opportunity to be regarded as our equals in the things of which they boast. 13 For such men are false apostles, deceitful workers, masquerading as apostles of Christ. 14 And no wonder, for Satan himself masquerades as an angel of light. 15 It is not surprising, then, if his servants masquerade as servants of righteousness. Their end*

will correspond to their actions.

Revelation 3:9 *I will make those who are of the synagogue of Satan, who claim to be Jews though they are not, but are liars—I will make them come and fall down at your feet and acknowledge that I have loved you.*

Well meaning men and women have had their good intentions manipulated by the master strategist's lies so that the whole world might go astray.

The purpose of this book is to present lies and scriptural truths about the very basic and important doctrines of Heavens King and Kingdom. I will be doing my very best not to call out any specific denomination or creed, but rather to help us understand that our enemy is NOT the church, but that Jesus wants His church back. The Spirit of God and the Word of Truth shall deliver us from the lie tactics of the Devil and his will to steal, kill, and destroy.

This book has been prayerfully and strategically written to this point in this progressive order:
Truth, Salvation, Righteousness, Faith, Love, Holy Spirit, Repentance, Commission; and to come, Dominion.

Please restrict every urge to skip ahead as you read.

Each chapter builds upon the establishment of previous principles.

As you read understand, these are not cute copy paste ideas to live by. This is war, real war. You are about to engage in seriously violent spiritual war against the Devil, a formidable strategist. He will try to lie to you the whole time. He will try to keep you from finishing the book. Fight hard, this is war.

6

WHICH WAY DO I RUN

Developing a sense of direction in life, war, or even sports requires fundamentals, practice, and experience. I've had the honor of coaching 7 seasons of soccer with my son as my star player. But he hasn't always been good at soccer. At age 4 he was afraid of the scrum. I know scrum is a rugby term, but lets be honest; is 4 year old soccer really much different from rugby? All 8 kids would travel in an amorphous blob chasing the ball. Sometimes the ball would pop out and one of our own kids would kick the ball towards the wrong goal. We would be screaming, "Go the other way! Wrong goal!" It's the result of inexperience. These kiddos are just doing their best according to their limited experience; and sometimes they score for the wrong team. We might laugh this off, but that's because we cannot truly call these kids 'soccer players' yet. They are just kids learning a new skill, my expectations are low at first. However 7 seasons in, my son is no longer expected to make these mistakes, but rather to play his position well and achieve the goals he aims for on the field.

I've never seen a four year old on ESPN being talked about for scoring in the wrong goal, but I have seen many clips of professionals doing so. The difference is in expectation and experience. The two go hand in hand. The more experience and acquired skill, the greater the expectation. It's all about the fundamentals. At higher levels of play, players are expected to have these fundamentals so deeply ingrained in them that they become first nature. When professionals miss on fundamentals, even those with little to no experience are entitled to their open criticism. This is the world we live in. People with limited knowledge, experience, and skill are professional commenters and critics on the best of the best. This is not only true of sports, but also business, government, education, ethics, and religion and the list goes on. These critics are given a false sense of superiority based on someone else's failure, not their own merit. This is the Devil's seat. He assumes a false sense of power from our failures, not from his merit – as Jesus Christ has stripped him of all authority. The enemy has two tactics, disqualify you on the merit of your own failures, or keep you from ever gaining the experience and knowledge to run in the right direction with the ball – in other words, he wants you playing in the wrong direction, kicking your ball into the wrong goals and celebrating it too. In doing so, you will have a false sense of achievement, all the while winning the award of the best player on the enemy's team. Your inexperience, and lack of understanding will lead to misdirection and continued failure. That my friend is the Devil's will at its core.

The goal is offensive, not defensive. Our goal is to score as many points as we can. The enemy doesn't have any offense of his own – only to turn your own team mates to the wrong goal. A well-trained team doesn't need to defend, it needs to score. You can never win a game without goals; the best you can do is tie at zeros. Now you might read this and say, "What about the armor of God, why would we need armor if we aren't playing defense." The answer is simple. The armor is just as offensive as it is defensive. Football pads protect a player, both in tackling and being tackled. The pads enable the player with the ball to run over or through his opponents without worry for the collision. It is for this reason that I will be using Ephesians 6 and the armor of God as the foundation for this teaching. I will help you understand the offense in the armor as God created it – the very things the Devil wills you to never understand.

The truth holds it all together. If the enemy wants to disarm you, then he has to get that belt of truth – everything else will fall off. Likewise, the truth is the best thing we have as an offense against the Devil. The truth sets you free, it isn't primarily a guard against captivity, it is primarily a weapon used against the chains of bondage. 'You shall know the truth, and the truth will set you free.' We must never forget this fact – Israel's battle didn't end with David conquering Goliath. The Israelite army took the offensive against the philistines driving them away creating many casualties against the enemy along the way. When you have been set free from an oppressive enemy, the defensive ought to become an after thought. Offense is the posture of one who has been set free. It is in that offensive pursuit that you reclaim every promise and territory that has been trampled on by the enemy. That sneaky snake knows if he can keep you on the defense that you'll never use your weapons against him, he will settle for a tie any day of the week – will you?

1 Timothy 3 tells us to flee the desires of the flesh. To flee from a lifestyle of sin. Many equate this to running from the Devil. This is not true. The word says we resist the Devil, draw near to God and the

Devil does the fleeing. That's a great plan. I like that one. Let's do that! The enemy wishes to keep you running away from Him all the while finding God and righteousness as unapproachable on the merit of your failures. Therefore we find ourselves homeless, trying to run away from selfish desires, but having no place to rest our souls. As long as righteousness is unattainable, the enemy wins, so the Devil convinces us that we are sinners and always will be. If God is unapproachable and righteousness is unattainable, we either flounder, or accept falleness as our nature and go live in the enemy's camp. We start kicking the ball in the wrong direction, as we flee God in 'reverence' for His holiness and embrace the nature of our enemy in the name of sound theology. This is how the enemy keeps us on the defensive, keeping God just beyond arms reach, while secretly scheming to escape the grasp of the evil desires of our flesh without embracing the freeing truth from the Spirit. He wants to keep us inexperienced, ineffective, and forgetting that we have been cleansed already of our sins. 2 Peter 1.

It isn't cute anymore to score in the wrong direction. The points count now, so learn to run in the right direction and score as many offensives as you can. Run in the direction of Jesus, draw near to Him and everything about Him. Pursue the Kingdom, righteousness, peace, and joy with all you are, and there you'll find true power. Romans 14:17 and 1 Cor. 4:20

You would be insane to run towards a goal you could never reach. *The Spirit God gives us is one of Power, Love, and a sound mind, or self-discipline.* 2 Timothy 1:7. Therefore we are equipped to aim at something achievable – and this is when many will slam the book shut. Righteousness is a real goal. It should be what we aim for. And not one of those 'I'd rather aim and miss, than not shoot' type things of either. Aiming and missing is sin. Sin is an archery term meaning – to miss. If you miss, you sin. This is where Romans 3:23 says *'all have sinned and fall short of the glory of God.'* Gods righteousness is the manifestation of the glory of His perfect character. This falling short implies that we not only aimed and missed, but also didn't even reach the target. The arrow didn't reach. This is where we start thinking that the righteousness of God is somehow unreachable. This is totally true in every carnal sense. No man, in himself has the capacity to even come close to righteousness in his own skill, strength or aim. But God calls us the righteousness of Christ. He says to put it on as a breastplate of righteousness. Either there is a paradox here, or righteousness isn't so hard to hit, let alone take hold of and wear. Is it possible that we all fall short of righteousness because we are attempting to shoot at a target while firing the opposite direction? It is not possible by every law of physics to shoot an arrow all the way around the world. By shooting west to hit an eastward target, we must traverse impossibility. But – if we shoot in the right direction, aim correctly, and allow Jesus to guide and empower us, the target becomes a very real possibility. You will never be righteous by aiming at your sin. You will only ever become righteous by making it the goal. Start shooting in the right direction. Start running in the right direction. Stop believing the lie that all of this is impossible. *For with God, nothing is impossible.* Matthew 19:26.

It's the Devil's will to keep you stuck on what is impossible with man, so that you never walk into what is possible with God. It's the Devil's will to confuse you about your purpose and power. It is the Devil's will to keep you believing lies that are so close to the truth that you actually believe the lie. The enemy masks himself, clothes himself in light, speaks from the very word of God, but everything that Devil says is a lie, it is his native language. John 8:44. The lies of the enemy are crafted in such a cunning way that they use the most credible truths to create the most believable of lies.

The deception from our enemy the Devil is so deep that many well meaning Christian leaders scream heresy at people who are simply speaking truth from Gods very word. This is the same form of persecution that Jesus suffered and He said, *"If they persecuted me, they will also persecute you."* John 15:20. Those that persecuted Jesus did it in the name of righteousness and under the accusation of heresy. Do not think for one minute that we are any different from Jesus. The greatest persecution of the truth happens in the church, not governments, nor other religions. The greatest persecution of the truth is coming from the inside. The Devil's will is to use the same tactics he used to kill Jesus, to kill the truth and the Holy Spirits operation in the body of Christ, which is the church. The Devil's will is to tell lies that sound like truths, so that the truth that sets you free sounds like a horrible heresy. What a sneaky snake our adversary has become.

The time has come for you to decide which way you will run. What is your goal? Make your goal Jesus, Christ alone, His Kingdom and His righteousness. Set your whole self to Him, and in doing so, you will disrupt the Devil's will.

THE TRUTH OF TRUTH

"A lie will go round the world while the truth is pulling its boots on"
~ Charles Spurgeon ~

"Go into all the world and preach the gospel to all creation"
Mark 16:15

The yo-yo is not a toy; it's a deadly weapon! I found this out first hand when my brother attempted to go around the world while standing two feet in front of me. One flick of the wrist and the next thing I knew, all was red. My eyebrow lost in the collision and blood was now streaming. I became hot with fury. It was only a flesh wound; I simply wished to return the favor in brotherly fashion. My brother dropped the yo-yo and ran, both from me, and to my parents. He wanted to make sure to do two things, tell his story first; and protect himself from my wrath. He was older than me by 13 months, but history had proven, before Jesus; I was a highly volatile explosive. This wouldn't be the first time my parents would have to tear me off of my brother in the middle of the living room floor.

This is the enemy's tactic. He knows what's coming to him, but if the Devil can tell the lie before you tell the truth, he can make your assault on him look more like a malicious and unwarranted hate crime, than exacting justice. The Devil's will is to place lies in front of you before you encounter the truth, and therefore make the truth look like a lie. The Devil does this to protect himself from your wrath. That's right I said that correctly. The Devil's will is to go ahead of you with lies to protect himself from your wrath. The lie he tells will sound like the truth; the best lies are the most believable ones. For instance "the yo-yo is a toy." Most assuredly I tell you, is not a toy. The yo-yo is a deadly primitive weapon. But we put these weapons in the hands of children and call them toys. We teach them to do tricks with them. They proudly go 'round the world and call the yo-yo a toy. The yo-yo is called a toy, and no longer used for its intended purpose. People laugh when you tell them it's a weapon. Can you think of anything else being used like a toy – for pleasure – to please people, contorted in many ways to present a pretty presentation? This weapon, the enemy puts into our hands, calls it a toy and exploits it for his satisfaction. This weapon is the word of God. *It is sharper than any two edged sword.* Hebrews 4:12. Please don't treat it like a toy, don't make it do neat tricks for others approval. Use it with focus– it tells the truth, the truth is our greatest offense and it holds everything together. When we yield the truth against the Devil, we crush his will and we demonstrate wrath and impending doom upon him. The Truth is not a toy, it is a deadly weapon. Its' the first thing the Devil wills to have you mistreat as a toy.

-Speaking your truth and the law of relativity.

'I'm a woman trapped in a man's body' – Speak your truth sister! Wait, what? Has something like truth become so relative? If truth is what you decide it is, than truth is simply opinion. People also accept it. 'It's their truth.' I know many are going to be upset by what I'm writing, but it's not my job to please people by misusing truth – if I did that, truth would be a toy, and not a weapon. I don't say this for my own satisfaction, but – Gods truth is the only truth. He himself is the truth, and if anything you think is true disagrees with God, you're surely deceived by the Devil's will. If you think God made a mistake in making you – you're the mistaken one and there is no truth in you. If this is you. You don't have the truth, speak nothing of the truth, and you need gentle instruction towards the truth. I hope you will come to your senses and escape the grasp of the Devil's will. 2 Timothy 2:25.

The law of relativity is really a perspective and comparison thing. I am big compared to an infant; I am small compared to an elephant. Truth relativism is the idea that things are only contextually or culturally true. The frame of reference changes and with it goes the truth. For instance the Silk worm: Most people know the silk worm for its ability to produce silk. It's a prized possession in many places to have a farm of silk worms. However in Korea the Silk worms pupae are eaten as street food called beondegi. Some call the silk worm a prized possession, some a material source and some call it food. In each instance we can call it true… however none of them are true. The truth is that a silk worm is a silk worm. That's the only truth; the created entity spoken into creation by God is the true thing. Its uses may vary, but the application of truth isn't truth. How you handle truth, is not truth – it's application. The environment you put truth in, the application you use truth for – this doesn't change the truth.

-A wrench is a wrench

I get overly creative sometimes. I don't know what my motivation is really; but sometimes I want to use a wrench as a hammer. Does that make the wrench a hammer? The wrench does the job of a hammer... kinda. Truth relativism would say, "By using a wrench to pound a nail, it becomes a hammer." Does this sound smart? Is this the function the wrench was made for? Do I seem like an intelligent *'creative,'* *(one who creates)* when I trade my hammer for a wrench? The fact is; I somehow convince myself that it is easier to use the tool in my hand for a purpose it wasn't designed for, than to go get the right tool. Apply relativity here. This is only true if I only have one nail to pound, as I can accomplish the job faster than if I were to go to the tool room and grab my hammer. The added variable is my skill level using a wrench as a hammer; embarrassingly, that skill level is increasing. Relativity also says if I have multiple nails to pound; I would not be intelligent or creative to continue misusing my wrench and calling it a hammer. Relativism can make a lot of sense, but truth relativity doesn't. To think my wrench is a hammer is a lie. Truth relativity is one way the Devil wills to have us believe lies about the weapons in our hands and the tools in our arsenal to build a case against him and deliver embarrassing defeat. We must learn what the truth is, how to use is, and what direction to apply it in. If truth is relative, it has no proper use, no direction, and no purpose — and therefore it becomes a dust collector on the shelf. Has your truth become a dust collector too?

Speaking my truth is only possible through one means: His truth is my truth. God is faithful and true. Jesus says He is the truth. John 14:6. If Jesus is the Truth, than I cannot speak truth unless it comes into alignment with who Jesus is, what Jesus is doing, or what Jesus is saying. Anything I call 'my truth' that doesn't agree with the Truth Jesus Christ, is simply a weak opinion. He is the eternal truth, constant, ultimate and absolute. I speak my truth when I tell His truth. The Devil's will is to confuse Jesus' words, character, and commission so that we don't walk in truth; but rather a form of truth that has been polluted by a lie, therefore rendering it untrue, weak, and fickle.

-Spinning Jenny and dress codes

Relativism has found its way into the church. I am only going to use one example; to use them all would be a deterrent from the theme of this book. Are you ready? Dressing your best means giving God your best! I get a kick out of the commonly shared idea that 'if you'll dress up for a date, why wouldn't you dress up for your date with Jesus?' People use this to somehow shame people into a cultural expression that has no root in the bible. Let me rephrase: The Devil expresses his will towards us by lying to us about what is acceptable to wear in order to approach God properly.

Please feel free to fact check me if this offends your sense of holiness. First off, the dress code in heaven is white robes, so get it right! Revelation 7:9. These white robes are those that have been washed by the overcoming blood of Jesus, Revelation 3:4-5, Revelation 7:14. These robes don't exist yet either. So I don't know what your feeble attempt from the Banana Republic is, but it's not in the Bible.

Let me school you a little on the history of dressing up for church. It's relatively new. In 1764 the Englishman James Hargreaves invented the spinning jenny. This was early in the industrial revolution and gave access to finer and lower cost clothing. What was reserved for only the most prestigious people now became accessible to the general public – fancy dress. John Wesley, in an attempt to keep classism from uprooting the church was a major opponent of the dress your best culture. He told people to dress down in humility; this allowed the poor not to be isolated and eventually pushed out by the posh culture of fancy dress, and the idolatry of the rich. Then came the rich and more liturgical movements. The staunch Anglicans and Presbyterians started encouraging dressing up – in doing so, they attracted wealthy people to fund their mission. In doing so, they evidently pushed everyone out that couldn't afford the nice clothes. The need to have a sense of belonging lead to people renting their suits and dresses for Sunday by leveraging their paychecks week by week. The leveraging of paychecks and constant rental kept the poor poorer and the rich getting richer. The fuel behind the dress your best culture was nothing more than idolatry and classism. Do you still want to dress up and call it your best? Or do you want to know the truth?

Hosea 4:6-7 *"My people are destroyed from lack of knowledge. "Because you have rejected knowledge, I also reject you as my priests; because you have ignored the law of your God, I also will ignore your children. The more priests there were, the more they sinned against me; they exchanged their glorious God for something disgraceful."*

The truth about the truth is that it only comes from God. Many men teach religion and church culture as truth. But these things are departures from Gods intended purpose for both the church and those who call themselves His. It is very possible that God has rejected a church that traded the truth for a lie. Traded the hammer of Gods truth for the wrench of relativism. Traded humility and brokenness for pride and cultural collectiveness. *My sacrifice is, O God, is a broken and contrite heart. You, God, will not despise.* Psalm 51:17. The church screams heresy every time the truth is preached over a popular church leaders complex explanation.

The truth is:

The truth is I am the righteousness of God in Christ Jesus, 2 Corinthians 5:21.

The truth is I can participate In Gods very nature and I have escaped the corruption in this world, 2 Peter 1:4.

The truth is I have been given a new nature and heart like Gods, Ezekiel 11:19 and 36:26.

The truth is my sin is removed from me as far as the east is from the west Psalm 103:12.

The truth is I am a brand new creation and I don't have to identify with what I used to be, for it is dead. 2 Corinthians 5:17

The truth is I am powerful and can do the same stuff Jesus did, even more than He did – John 14:12

I have the power of decree in heaven and earth –

Matthew 18:18

The truth is: none of these truths are possible unless Christ lives in and through you as LORD and King. A cute little 'repeat after me' prayer and a raised hand don't cut it. The Devil's will is to make leaders into oppressors of the truth. Without this oppression of truth; people would experience a greater presence and power from God than the leader they are supposed to be following. The leader would lose his career and church followership. So the Devil uses church leaders at the merit of their failures to leak lies to the people that they cannot be like Jesus, but remain sinners, powerless and hopeless. Playing defense until death conquers them because; after all, their leader is powerless, yet more spiritual than they are. So, the leader echoes the Devil, shouts of heresy come from their lips. The deception is so deep; they actually think they are doing the LORDS work in exposing the enemy and disassociating. Ephesians 5:11.

The righteousness, which is supposed to be inherent to those who believe, has been traded for relativism through prideful self-righteousness. Let me explain. The Devil's will is for us to believe relativism truth trumps biblical truth.

Relativism says, "My life experience has been that I am not righteous, therefore I cannot be righteous."

Relativism says: I have never seen anyone get healed, so I can't do the things Jesus did.

Relativism says: "I still struggle with sin, so I must be a sinner and not a saint."

Relativism says: "I don't feel very new, I must not be a new creation."

Relativism is the voice of the Devil's will speaking lies that sound so believable that the truth, the only truth is disregarded. Well-meaning leaders, out of presumptuous pride make these statements to disqualify the truth of God in order to qualify themselves as truth bringers. This is the deepest persecution of the truth I have found in the world today. Truth is truth in every situation, it never loses, and Jesus never loses. Jesus is the Truth. Jesus is not relative, He is absolute. And a wrench is a wrench, not a hammer.

There is one truth to relativism: In Christ, I am just like Him in every way. Apart from Christ, I am not. Consider this truth when considering who the real heretics are. I will wield the truth as a weapon against the Devil's will, not as a toy for entertainment. Will you?

Last week during our testimony time in a church meeting; a woman told a story about God's faithfulness but mentioned her knee getting injured somewhere in the story. She was going to go to the doctor the next day and could hardly walk on it. The whole church body was listening to her testimony, they applauded Jesus at the end of the testimony and she began to walk back down the isle. I paused her and said to the whole church, "I don't believe it's Gods will for her to stay injured. I need women full of the Spirit to come lay hands and pray." Within fifteen seconds a dozen or so women were making Heavens decree. They were not asking God to do something He already did; they were making the Decree according to God's will. The woman saw some immediate relief and was well the next morning. She never needed to go to the doctors; she needed to just go to church! I know the truth; God bought her healing with His wounds. Knowing the truth empowers the prophetic decree and miracles just happen. I am so proud of the people I get to serve who know they can declare truth with power and confidence. Jesus shows up when we agree with His truth. It's time to see Him show up with increase as you come into alignment with Truth and reject the lie tactics of the Devil's will.

WHEN IS A PIZZA DELIVERED?

Disclaimer: This is not an attempt to reconcile the 'can you lose your salvation' or 'once saved always saved' argument. I am neither a Calvinist nor an Armenian. I am a follower of Jesus Christ, not a subscriber to mans ideas about God. If you don't know what a Calvinists or Armenians are you're probably better off for that. Essentially they are differing camps of theology that happen to each see from the limited perspective of a man. Most people identify with one over the other, however neither tells the whole story as God would tell it. 1 Corinthians 3:4 *"When one of you says, "I am a follower of Paul," and another says, "I follow Apollos," aren't you acting just like people of the world?"* Both Paul and Apollos were pretty cool people to follow, but plug in Calvinism and Armenianism in for Paul and Apollos and you'll catch my drift, smells good don't it. It's worldly, limited, and insufficient.

The Devil wills to keep us in the dark about what salvation actually is. Ask someone 'what is salvation?'... Go on. Ask them. I'll wait. Put this book down and ask someone. Can't find anyone? Ask yourself, and note well your answer. Give it time to settle.

....
....
....
....
....
....
....
....
....
....
....
....
....
....
....

The trouble with writing a book is I sort of have to guess what the answers might be and give a blind and slightly educated response. Most people will have a response that sounds like: "Salvation means I am going to heaven instead of hell." Or "Jesus paid the debt I owed because of my sin." There is nothing wrong with these statements. Both are factual statements of those who have experienced Jesus. For Jesus is salvation. He is Savior. There is so much more to salvation than a ticket to heaven, and a punishment passed on. The Devil's will is to keep us believing lies about complete salvation, so we never allow salvation to empower us to leave the Devil's bondage and lying rhetoric.

Salvation in Hebrew meant simply 'deliverance' but in the Greek, as Jesus' disciples proclaimed it would have been *soteria*, meaning: Deliverance from the molestation of the enemy, Security, and the sum of every benefit and promise of the Kingdom of Heaven. I will attempt to take each of these identifiers and bring the context of Gods salvation to a tangible reality.

-When is the Pizza saved?

Peter was asked in Acts 2:37-38 'what should we do that we might be saved?' and He said to 'repent and be baptized.' In a later chapter I will cover repentance in depth. For now just understand repentance has much more to do with agreeing with God about everything than simply disagreeing with sin and doing your best to quit failing at life. Baptism is an act of will and obedience, and I'll leave that one for another time as well. Let me tell you what didn't happen. Peter didn't have an altar call with every head bowed and eyes closed. He didn't shout, "I see that hand" three thousand times to acknowledge those who were being saved that day. Salvation is something so much deeper than a prayer.

Salvation is worked out in *fear and trembling*, Philippians 2:12. As we agree with God about everything it should create a fearfulness that if we don't we won't experience the deliverance promised and the reality of God's dominion now on earth as it is in heaven. But what fear? Why tremble if Jesus loves you. *There is no fear in love for fear has to do with judgment*. 1 John 4:18. I am simply afraid to miss something amazing. In the words of Steven Tyler, 'I don't want to miss a thing.' I am afraid of less than complete deliverance, and therefor I yield it all to Jesus, keeping nothing of myself to myself. This deliverance occurs through repentance. As you agree with truth, you are delivered from the paralyzing lie of the enemy.

So when is the pizza saved? Some would argue there is no saving of pizza. I argue otherwise. The pizza is saved when it's delivered. Before the pizza was delivered, it was a slave to the baker. The baker sold the pizza for a price to someone who would appreciate it, consume it, and make it part of themselves. The pizza is delivered, not when it gets to your door. The pizza is fully delivered when its nutrients enter the bloodstream of the one who designed it for their own purpose and use. The pizza was delivered from the baker, to the true maker and designer. I call it the deep-dish truth about Salvation.

Salvation is not a possession; it's a position in the person of Jesus. You don't get saved, you enter into salvation. Isaiah 12:2 says, *"Surely God is my salvation, I will trust and not be afraid. The LORD, the LORD Himself, is my strength and my defense, He has become my salvation."* David describes the salvation of the LORD in Psalm 61 as his refuge, a tower of strength, a fortress. Salvation is a position in a person, and that person is Jesus. Salvation is not an item you gain like a golden ticket to Wonka's chocolate factory. Salvation is the promise and presence of Jesus. It is deliverance from the lies and the presence of the enemy. It is impossible to be delivered FROM the Devil, and not TO Jesus. We must be assimilated into the person of Christ, covered by His DNA, His blood, positioned in the Kingdom of heaven, with heavens promise and resource all around us.

Salvation is not simply having your name written in

the book of life, or a safe hall pass signed by Peter. The book of life already has everyone's name in it; names are blotted out, not added. Revelation 3:5 *'The one who is victorious will be dressed in white. And I will never blot out his name from the book of life, but I will confess his name before My Father and His angels."* Salvation is much less having something added to your life, it is much more about walking into what Jesus has already purchased and prepared for you. Deliverance happens when Jesus purchases you from the Devil and brings you into himself. The Pizza is delivered when it enters the bloodstream, and you are delivered when you live in and through Jesus.

Jesus didn't purchase your sins, He purchased you. Salvation is not freedom from your sins wages, Salvation is new residency in Christ, fully delivered from the chains of bondage that the Devil's lies kept you bound by. Jesus bought you with a price, Therefore *Honor God with your body* and *do not become a slave of man* ever again. 1 Corinthians 6:20 and 7:23. When Jesus bought you, He made his dwelling place with you so that He alone could enjoy you and you would enjoy Him. He didn't buy your sin from you so you could enjoy your life. He bought you so that His joy might be made complete in and through you. The Devil's will is to make you think that salvation is a possession that can be earned, lost, or redeemed like a ticket. The truth is Salvation is a position in Christ. Christ is Savior and outside of Him there is no Salvation to be found. We have literally been delivered from the evil one to the righteous one. A pizza is saved when it enters the bloodstream, Salvation happens when we are positioned wholly and fully in Christ alone.

-Roller coasters are freaky and thrillin

One day at an amusement park for my family of four can cost me a week's wages. For some reason we always think it's worth it though. I forget what I paid for a ride while I'm flying upside down at 60 miles per hour. But the fact is this. The ride is like 2 minutes long and I wait in line for 2 hours to ride with my hands surrendered while screaming like a little girl. I scream because its fun, like a little girl because its funny, I'm not scared, really. Judge me; go ahead, I know what I'm talking about.

My favorite rides are the ones where you are literally dangling from the harness like the piece of pistachio currently hanging out in the back of my throat. I should chew more thoroughly. These dangling coasters are freaky and thrilling. I have to put absolute trust in the security of the harness in order to have a good time. How do you know my trust is absolute? If I didn't trust the harness absolutely, I'd be willing to die for a ride, I am staking my life and well being on a harness while I fly as high and my girly screams ascend higher still. It's the illusion of fear coupled with the real security of the harness that make the ride fun.

Life is a roller coaster with all its ups and downs, twists and surprises. Salvation is that security harness. Tell me, would a roller coaster be more fun if you were not strapped into the harness? (Someone is saying yes, and they need to get their head checked.) The harness of security in Christ is Salvation, Christ Himself cradling you in his strong arms. It isn't any safer to attempt life without Jesus than to go on one of those dangling death traps without a harness. It isn't any more fun to attempt to do so as some might imply. Life with Jesus is secure, even in death. Life with Jesus is more fun too. His security allows you to have joy in the middle of the greatest drops, dips, twists and surprises in life. The more extreme the roller coaster, the greater the harness build, the more I need to rely on it. It is possible that many of us haven't left the kiddy section of life's roller coaster section because you don't need a harness on those rides. Playing it super safe is also super boring. People who live this way never experience the freaky thrill of

Salvations security through any and every trial.

Life without Jesus is downright scary. Just like an extreme coaster without a security harness, life is petrifying without Salvation. If you are calling yourself a follower of Jesus Christ, yet living in perpetual fear, the Devil has you in his will. In John 10:10 Jesus says He came so that we might enjoy life and have it to the full or in abundance. Tell me that kiddy coaster is abundant life because you're scared of anything else and I'll introduce you to the most thrilling and secure ride of your life – Jesus' Salvation. Joy is perhaps one of the most evident fruits of God's Holy Spirit because Joy is had when we are secure through trials in Christ our Salvation. So test your harness out, scream like a 6-year-old girl if you have to. Just make sure you have fun while Jesus hangs on to you. He isn't going to let go; He isn't a puny God.

The Devil's will is to keep you on the kiddy coaster. The Devil wants to bore your faith to death. He wants you to never trust in Jesus enough to stake your life or well being on the greatest and most costly adventure you can ever go on. It's called absolute trust in the Security of Christ. He paid a high price to get you in, are you sure all you wanna do is ride the kiddy coasters. The Devil's will is to keep you on that same boring coaster and afraid of anything that requires absolute trust. He wants you to believe the lie that Jesus could drop you at any point during that ride and it'll ruin your ride, it'll keep joy far from you, and your screams will be for help, not of joy.

-Unworthy and Unwealthy

Lets assume the owner of a chain of Hobby Lobby stores asks you a very simple question: I picked Hobby Lobby because for many, it's kinda like heaven on earth. They take you to one of their Hobby Lobby locations and as you pull in they say, "You can have anything you want, just say the word." What would you pick? Would you look for the most expensive item you could only dream about? Would you go middle of the road to express your gratitude without greed? Would you go for the pack of gum in the checkout isle in display of humility? Think about it. You can have anything; just pick it out. I think Jesus proposes the same thing when He says, *"ask and it will be given, seek and you will find, knock and the door will be opened."* Matthew 7:7. And again He says, *"Ask anything in my name and I will do it."* John 14:14. How do you even respond to that?

Have you come up with what you'd ask for from Hobby Lobby? Ask for anything and it's yours. What's your answer? I'll tell you mine. I wouldn't ask for anything in the store. I'd ask for the store. I don't want to live my life thinking I'm only deserving of the pack of gum in heavens pantry. Nor thinking I can only have one truly valuable gift from heaven. I mean it when I pray for His Kingdom to come on earth as it is in Heaven. If I'm being asked what I want in heaven: I want it all, I want it all here on earth as it is in Heaven. This isn't heresy, it's Jesus' prayer style and it's the role Salvation plays on earth. Every manifestation of Heaven on earth is another slap in the Devil's face and another exploit against his will. The Devil's will is to keep you begging for the pack of gum and calling yourself unworthy of it. I am satisfied with nothing less than heaven on earth. Salvation is Heaven on earth as well as heaven in heaven.

When people ask me, "What's your spiritual gift?" I really just want to say "All of them." Remember, I'm asking for the whole store. We must fully understand that living in the deliverance, security, and provision of Jesus means accepting nothing less than complete Salvation. Now Salvation truly is the Spiritual gift in every conceivable way. The Devil's will is to keep you from ever asking for more than the pack of gum and a ride on the kiddy coaster. It's Gods will that you ask for the fullness of heaven on earth and that my friend is the freaky and thrilling truth about salvation.

-You are on an undefined diet

If Salvation itself exists in the person of Christ, and in order to participate in complete deliverance, security, and heavens resource; we have to ask ourselves a very real question… 'What is Jesus' diet?'

One of my favorite meals in the world is baked fish with brown rice and steamed veggies. A little salt and pepper and I'm happy. Put that next to a big mac and I'll pick the fish every time. When given the choice, I identify my default diet. An effective diet is a matter of preferences, not restrictions. Likewise, a bad diet is also a matter of preferences. Put little Debbie, any little Debbie treat next to a piece of fruit and I will probably pick Debs, she's been with me through a lot y'all. This is a bad diet choice, a developed preference of mine. I truly want it see this preference change. Both good and bad diet choices are a matter of preference. At least in first world nations it is. If I put baked fish and brown rice next to little Debbie snacks. I'll pick the fish and rice by a small margin y'all. The struggle is real.

1 Corinthians 10:23 *"All things are lawful, but not all things are profitable. All things are lawful, but not all things edify."*

Lets assume I have a goal. I'm going to gain 20 pounds of muscle and lose 10 pounds of fat. Basically that's every man in the world's goal. What should I eat? There will be differing opinions on how to achieve the goal, but none of the diets to achieve this goal include eating nothing but little Debbie snacks. I am positive of that much. Achieving the goal would require me to adjust my preferences, and then to hope the preferences stick after. When the preferences finally stick in the right way, it's called lifestyle change. When my appetite is Jesus, and whatever He craves; that's nature change.

Jesus is God and God is limitless. Jesus does not live within the parameters of restrictions. Jesus thrives because His perfect will always chooses the best preference. Jesus doesn't have a hard time deciding between wickedness and goodness – His perfect nature craves goodness. For Jesus goodness and wickedness aren't like nutritious meals versus junk food. Goodness is like good food, and wickedness is doggy do dew. When was the last time you licked your chops while watching a dog do its duty? Congratulations, you have established your first healthy preference – that which edifies and builds up over that which doesn't.

Jesus has prepared a table for you. Don't bring a bag

lunch.   My wife and I have the privilege of having new families at our table as often as possible. We always ask if there are any food allergies or special diets and prepare accordingly. I can recall a few times when parents have shown up with children and a sack lunch. The food I cooked was delicious, but the kid will only eat mac n cheese and chicken nuggets. It wasn't an insult to me because it was a child. But what if it was an adult. What if the people I invited over brought their own PB n J to the table. Let's take it a notch further, what if they gathered my dogs poop from the yard and brought it in as if to say, "Why would you leave the good stuff in the grass?" How would I respond? How much would my heart break for them that they are more satisfied with THAT! I would feel rejected to a point. Apply this when you sit at Jesus' table. Salvation has supplied the food for a fruitful and abundant life. It's time for a diet change. Salvation is sitting at the table of the LORD.

It takes 30 days to develop a new habit. Taste buds change every 10-14 days. This means, good eating habits change through repetition which produces a new acquired taste. In the same way – we have to *taste and see that the LORD is good* Psalm 34:8. Our preference for sin is like growing up eating fecal matter and developing a preference for that which we have only ever known. Jesus has a different diet; one that builds you and fills you up. Jesus feasts on the fruit of Heaven. Salvation is having access to all of Heavens fruits. They will fill you and satisfy you as they do the same for Jesus. These fruits are: *Love, Joy, Peace, Patience, Kindness, Goodness, Faithfulness, Gentleness, and Self-Control.* Galatians 5:22-23. The fruit of His diet is the result of what He calls His food: *'to do the will of the one who sent me and to finish His work.'* John 4:34. We cannot have the amazing fruit of Heaven apart from complete obedience to the will of God.

Salvation is nature change. He has rescued us from the diet of the sin nature and given us a new one by Salvation. Galatians 5:24-25 *'Those who belong to Christ Jesus have nailed the passions and desires of their sinful nature to His cross and crucified them there. Since we are living by the Spirit, let us follow the Spirit's leading in every part of our lives.'* Also 2 Peter 1:4 explains it like this: *'and because of His glory and excellence, He has given us great and precious promises. These are the promises that enable you to share His divine nature and escape the world's corruption caused by human desires.'* The new nature is not 'like' Gods, it IS His nature. His nature consists of every preference we need to constantly choose what is best to build up His Kingdom.

Salvation means, a new diet. Salvation is Jesus. To live and move in Him. Salvation means His diet becomes your diet, because His resources become your resources. Salvation is not a ticket to Heaven; it is the person and the presence of Jesus. Salvation is not only a hope, but also security for life's best rides. Salvation is not a thing, but provision for all things in Christ. Salvation is nature change. Salvation is so much more than a prayer – that's just the starting place.

The Devil's will is to keep you believing Salvation is so much less than it is. The Devil wants you to believe you're still in bondage to sin. The Devil is okay with you calling salvation a hope for what is to come as long as you don't enter the promise on earth. Salvation has already broken every chain of bondage and called you free from the Devil's lies, it's time to embrace this truth and walk hand in hand with Jesus out of the prison the Devil wills to keep you in. Salvation is here, Salvation is Jesus, and Salvation is now.

THE TROJAN HORSE

Righteousness in the Greek: Dikaiosyne
The broad and narrow of it all. In a broad sense righteousness is the state of him who is, as he ought to be, righteousness, the condition acceptable to God. In a narrower sense, justice or the virtue which gives each his due.

-Trojan Horses
I am writing this book on a mac book pro laptop. Every time I push a key, it sends specific binary code through the computers inner parts. I wish I could tell you I am an expert at understanding everything about how this process works, but I don't. It doesn't bother me one bit either. Everything is as it should be and I like it that way. This is called righteousness. The moment this computer doesn't do what I tell it to, the computer is no longer righteous; it no longer is working according to its design.

In 2015 Apple hired 2 hackers that created an undetectable virus for mac. The Devil is attempting to feed undetectable viruses into our mindset, our operating system. The difference is, instead of hiring him; Jesus has turned Him into his personal footstool. Apple has built a reputation for itself for having a much more secure operating system than other developers. This reputation holds especially true when you use a computer for what it was designed for and stay off them websites you weren't designed for.

Can you guess what the operating system of your life is? From it flows every action, both voluntary and involuntary. Your mind. Your mind is the operating system for your life. Your mind is where the Devil plants his virus so that you don't operate the way you were made to operate. The Devil wants you to believe that righteousness is meant for anything but you. The Devil wants to keep you blind to the intention of righteousness in your life. The virus is the lie that you cannot be righteous. The virus is the lie that righteousness is something it is not. The lie is that you need to be okay with not being righteous. Furthermore the lie is that you must prosecute those who claim righteousness as heretics. The virus has penetrated the operating system of many believers, so much so that it has infiltrated nearly every church body. Such a sneaky virus goes by no other name but the Trojan horse of the Devil's will.

I know a little bit about computers, but my knowledge seems to wane as time goes by and advancements are made. As of the writing of this: one of the most deadly types of malware you can get is a *Trojan horse*. Now these sneaky little guys open the door for other viruses to get in under the guise of helpful software. Trojan horses are imposters that claim to be healthy for your computer, when in reality they attack healthy components and invite multiplying viruses in the back door. This is the Devil's will. To plant bad doctrine in your life, tell you it'll make life better, all the while rendering you ineffective and overloaded by junk.

The original Trojan horse story seals the end of a 10-year attack on the city of Troy by the Greeks. The Greeks were unable to penetrate the city walls for ten years. The solution was to build a giant horse and put their most valiant warriors inside of it, then to offer it as a gift to the city of Troy. Their most valiant warrior Odysseus was selected to lead the warriors inside the horse. It worked. The Greeks managed to completely destroy the city of Troy under the cleaver guise of a grand gift gesture. The Devil knows this tactic too. The Devil's will is to package his most malicious lies as a gift to the church. The Devil wants to disarm and destroy Gods people from the inside out. Look around. Do you see it happening? The Odysseus in the Devil's Trojan horse is this nasty lie – you will never be righteous, and you'll always be a sinner. The Devil's will is for you to believe this as good wisdom and not a lie. The Devil's will is to keep you from ever being 'as you should be' righteous. The moment you accept not being as you should be, as you were designed by God to be; you open the door to what should not be. That my friend is the Devil's will.

Funny how we live in a world that rejects righteousness yet wants to believe everything is as it should be in their life. As we reject righteousness we open the door for the counterfeit, a false sense that things are already as they were designed to be.

-Acceptable as I should be
Genesis 1:27-31 *"So God created human beings in his own image.*

In the image of God he created them; male and female he created them.

28 Then God blessed them and said, "Be fruitful and multiply. Fill the earth and govern it. Reign over the fish in the sea, the birds in the sky, and all the animals that scurry along the ground."

29 Then God said, "Look! I have given you every seed-bearing plant throughout the earth and all the fruit trees for your food.

30 And I have given every green plant as food for all the wild animals, the birds in the sky, and the small animals that scurry along the ground—everything that has life." And that is what happened.

31 Then God looked over all he had made, and he saw that it was very good!
And evening passed and morning came, marking the sixth day.

Scripture must weigh more heavily than our life experiences. Genesis 1 tells us of the intent of creation. God made man in His image for the purpose of community and dominion. God chose His image because He also gave us His responsibility. The dominion God gave Adam in the garden was a special one. The garden was the starting place – the whole world was the goal. Perfect righteousness is seen when God looks over all He made and called it very good. Everything was as it should be. The Devil's will is to steal the intended purpose of our design from us by telling lies. When we believe the lie, we empower the liar.

-The shot heard around the world

Debate still surrounds the events on April 19 1775 – the birth of the American Revolution. The shot heard around the world is commonly referred to as the

Americans first volley at the North Bridge Skirmish in Concord Massachusetts. The British would lose the battles of Lexington and Concord that day. Earlier that same day in Lexington, British soldiers killed Eight Americans. The question still remains as to who actually started the war. Was it the British in Lexington, or the Americans at the North Bridge? I can say this confidently; the British generated the first casualties in Lexington and the Americans retaliated later that day. This is what it looks like to start a war. The whole known world felt the revolution, and today the United States has risen as one of the greatest world powers, far exceeding Britain.

The Devil cast the first casualties in the Garden when he planted deadly lies in Eve's head. The Devil used the truth mixed with a lie to deceive Eve, then Adam as well. He said, "you will not die" which was the lie, mixed with the truth that 'God knows you will be like Him knowing good and evil.' The name of the tree was the tree of the knowledge of good and evil. The Devil's will was to take common information and use it to cause distrust. It worked. Eve then saw the fruit of the tree for what it was. The fruit was good for food, for gaining wisdom, and pleasing to the eye. Genesis 3:6. The Devil's will is to make anything that destroys righteousness look like the good stuff that's being withheld. The issue is, the Devil's will is also to blind us through lies to the repercussion of choosing that which we ought not partake in. The Devil's will is to keep us far away from our purpose, because our purpose includes taking dominion back from him.

The Devil wants to keep his casualties without the revolution. The retaliation is as such '*He will crush your head, and you will bruise His heel.*' Genesis 3:15. This was the first prophecy about Christ. Christ came to crush the crooked snakes head. The bruised heel points to the best the Devil could do, the cross. When we allow the purpose of God to be restored to our lives, we move towards true righteousness. We move towards our purpose, and this in fact gives the Devil a headache. The lies told in the garden were the shots heard around the world – but a louder cry was heard at the cross, where the revolution was birthed.

Jesus life, death, and resurrection were not simply for a promise of what's to come in heaven. Jesus came to restore our purpose for righteousness, so that we might be those who are as we should be – acceptable to God for His good work.

-The fear of temptation

Righteousness is not avoiding temptation. Immediately following Jesus' baptism, He was led into the wilderness by the Holy Spirit to be tempted.

Jesus didn't avoid temptation, He overcame it.

Someone recently told me they hadn't met anyone righteous before, and if that person exists, they probably live in absolute isolation to maintain their righteousness. Righteousness isn't avoiding temptation or the potential for failure. Righteousness is functioning according to the good design and perfect will of God. If righteousness were equated to seclusion and inactivity, Righteousness would be a loss of purpose and design. I would find myself emulating a rock instead of the rock of my salvation.

The idea of righteousness being the act of fearfully doing nothing is covered in the parable of the talents in Matthew 25:19-30. There were three servants in the parable. Two invested what was given and saw increase. One did nothing out of fear of failing. The fate of the one who did nothing but hide had a very fearful fate. *'Throw the bad servant out into the darkness. There will be loud crying and grinding of teeth.''* Matthew 25:30. If righteousness were attained through seclusion, this servant would have been praised. However God created us to increase. To be 'fruitful and multiply' His Kingdom and dominion on earth as it is in Heaven. This is the goal of righteousness; the Devil's will is that you never do anything more than hole up and wait for your impending doom. The Devil will call you righteous while you wait for disaster.

Have you ever gotten stage fright? You know that moment when everything you've been preparing for comes to a head. People's expectations are high and suddenly your confidence plummets. Your voice stops working, your heart beats hard, flushing your face red and warm. I've been there, but I'm not going back. I don't get nervous before I preach or sing anymore. I'm going to share the secret with you. Trust the work God is doing. That's it. Trust what God is doing. Do not, I repeat, do not trust wholly in your preparation or skill. Just trust in what God is doing.

Psalm 23:4 *"Even though I walk through the darkest valley, I will fear no evil, for you are with me; your rod and your staff, they comfort me."*

Trust Him. Trust His presence. Trust that if you are doing what you were designed to do, He is there eradicating fear. If you 'are as you should be' according to righteousness: He is the *'I am, that I am'* you need. Exodus 3:14

It is impossible to be living in Salvation and not enter righteousness. Remember Salvation is to Christ and rescued from the enemy. Salvation is security. Salvation is access to all of the promises and resources in Christ. Salvation is found when we are placed in the person and presence of Jesus. To claim salvation without righteousness is to claim homelessness and purposelessness. Heaven is come; the Kingdom is your residency. Your purpose can be fulfilled; the provision is already supplied in Christ. Your place and purpose are Salvation and Righteousness. The Devil's will is to keep you homeless and purposeless by believing you cannot be as you were designed to be. You were designed in Gods image, to reign like Him, to see His Kingdom increase on earth as it is in heaven. You must do this in righteousness.

-Getting what's due me

Justice means 'to restore the standard.' The Hebrew word for righteousness has 'Justice' as its primary function. Justice is restoring the standard, in other words: putting things back as they should be. Righteousness takes justice a step further to make provision for what is owed. But owed by whom and for what? I find it very possible that righteousness has a second edge to it; one the Devil wills for us to never discover. It's the law of restitution. Exodus 22:7 tells us a caught thief must pay back double. The Devil comes to steal, kill, and destroy. The Devil seeks to steal every gift God gives you. The Devil's will is that you never become righteous, because when you do the Devil must repay double what he took. This is especially true on the account of Job receiving a double portion after the Devil took so much from him. Grasping righteousness not only restores the standard, but also increases the standard restored at the expense of the thief.

What Is due to you? Let's start with the first repercussion of the fall in the garden. Genesis 3:7 'Then the eyes of both of them were opened, and they realized they were naked; so they sewed fig leaves together and made coverings for themselves.' The first repercussion of the fall was shame. The Devil wants to keep shame governing your life. What is owed to you is a double portion of innocence and joy. Righteousness cannot coexist in the mind of a man who believes he is corrupt.

Nehemiah 8:9-12 *Then Nehemiah the governor, Ezra the priest and teacher of the Law, and the Levites who were instructing the people said to them all, "This day is holy to the Lord your God. Do not mourn or weep." For all the people had been weeping as they listened to the words of the Law.*
10 Nehemiah said, "Go and enjoy choice food and sweet drinks, and send some to those who have nothing prepared. This day is holy to our Lord. Do not grieve, for the joy of the Lord is your strength."
11 The Levites calmed all the people, saying, "Be still, for this

is a holy day. Do not grieve."
12 Then all the people went away to eat and drink, to send portions of food and to celebrate with great joy, because they now understood the words that had been made known to them.'

The Devil's will is to keep you shameful weeping, powerless, and malnourished when the Word of God is presented to you. But the Joy of the LORD is your strength. The Devil knows that as long as you are shameful, constantly reminded of failure, you are weak. The double portion of strength is on its way for those who are ready to be restored by righteousness.

The first thing God wants to do is restore the standard of purity in your life. When Isaiah encountered God he said *'woe to me, I am ruined, I am a man of unclean lips.'* Immediately a coal from the altar was brought to cleanse his lips. From that point on Isaiah spoke with two pure voices: His own and Gods. This was the double portion owed. Righteousness is putting things back as they should be, restoring the standard and empowering the purpose.

Righteousness came to the leper that returned to worship Jesus after he was healed.
Luke 17:11-19 *As Jesus continued on toward Jerusalem, he*

reached the border between Galilee and Samaria. ₁₂ As he entered a village there, ten men with leprosy stood at a distance, ₁₃ crying out, "Jesus, Master, have mercy on us!"

₁₄ He looked at them and said, "Go show yourselves to the priests." And as they went, they were cleansed of their leprosy.

₁₅ One of them, when he saw that he was healed, came back to Jesus, shouting, "Praise God!" ₁₆ He fell to the ground at Jesus' feet, thanking him for what he had done. This man was a Samaritan.

₁₇ Jesus asked, "Didn't I heal ten men? Where are the other nine? ₁₈ Has no one returned to give glory to God except this foreigner?" ₁₉ And Jesus said to the man, "Stand up and go. Your faith has made you whole (sozo)."

Jesus spoke the word 'sozo' to the leper who returned to Him. All 10 lepers were healed. All 10 were delivered from their sickness. Only one was made whole. The sozo word is the restoration of righteousness. It is impossible to be restored as you should be apart from worship that is up close and personal. The sozo word was spoken when the leper threw himself at Jesus feet. Before this, the lepers cried out from a distance. The healing took place as they obeyed Christ's instruction. Sozo wholeness happens in close proximity to Jesus. If we are constantly aware of what separates us from God; sin, we never truly draw close enough to be made as we should be, to have the standard restored and live righteous.

Righteousness cannot be imparted from a distance. Jesus must close the proximity just like the coal to the lips, or throwing ourselves at His feet. The Devil wants to keep us pushing Jesus away because of our sin. You are no better than Peter when he said *'Go away from me lord for I am a sinful man.'* Luke 5:8. Jesus almost ignored the statement and simply said, *'Do not be afraid, from now on you will fish for men.'* Luke 5:10. Peter met Jesus with a great awareness of his sinfulness. Peter was so aware of his own sin that he instantly disqualified himself. Jesus was so aware of Peters purpose that he cast off shame and fear, and hewn destiny upon Peter. The Devil's will is for us to believe righteousness will reject us, but the reality is; righteousness restores us.

I know by now someone is remembering Romans 3:10 *'There is no one who is righteous, not even one.'* This reference to Psalm 14 by Paul in Romans is the singular justification used by so many to answer why they cannot be righteous. This is where context becomes highly critical. This verse was used by Paul to explain why we ought to be righteous, justified by Christ. He is explaining why we cannot embrace the sin nature, but rather take hold of what Christ has done through His own justification and righteousness. Read all of Romans 3 and 4 to get the full context. Romans 3:11 also says nobody seeks God, But here are a few of more than 20 promises for seekers:

Jeremiah 29:13 'You will seek me and you will find me with all your heart.'
Matthew 5:6 'God blesses those who hunger and thirst for righteousness,
  for they will be satisfied.
Matthew 7:7 Ask and it will be given to you; seek and you will find; knock and the door will be opened to you.
Amos 5:4 This is what the Lord says to Israel: "Seek me and live".

We cannot use Romans 3 out of context with the whole word to disqualify righteousness, to do so we would have to disqualify every effort to seek God. We would have to disqualify every blessing in order to disqualify righteousness. Do yourself a favor and quit playing into the Devil's will. The Devil's will is to get you to disarm and disqualify the promises of God for yourself. To keep God at a distance, and therefore your purpose is always far from you.

The truth about righteousness is that we might not understand how it works any more than we understand our computers inner workings. Righteousness is the goal of Christ in your life.

Righteousness is having the standard restored in your life so you can live out your God intended purpose. If your purpose in life is righteousness, then your purpose is not sinfulness. Make a decision today whom you will agree with, Christ and His righteousness, or the Devil and his sinfulness. Righteousness means becoming just as God intended you to be and nothing less. Righteousness means getting what's coming to you in the inheritance of Heaven and the repayment from the evil one. Righteousness is the abundant life Jesus said He came to bring us. Sozo healing is at the feet of Jesus. It's the Devil's will for you to keep God at a distance.

INFOMERCIALS AND TOKENS

'In addition to all of this, take up the shield of faith, with which you can extinguish all the flaming arrows of the evil one.'
Ephesians 6:16

I love my kids. Because I love my children I give them the best gifts, the best of my time, the best of myself. My kids look like me a bit. People often tell them how quickly they recognize whose they are… they smile with pride; this is a good thing. There have been hilarious cases of mistaken identity as well. I think we have all had them; the 'your baby is so cute' followed by flushed cheeks, 'Oh, no this kid isn't mine, I'm just holding it.' Children tend to look more and more like their parents as they grow and mature.

Faith is the growth and maturation agent in our lives. It can be very difficult to tell a brand new saint from a mature sinner. It's the Devil's will to keep you defined as his and unrecognizable as a Son of God from a son of rebellion. Faith, and the evidence of faith in your life become the great indicator of whose you truly are.

My children don't doubt who their daddy is. They look in the mirror and they see me. My children look at how I love them and they see their daddy. My children look at my provision for them in every way and they see their daddy. My children look at how I sacrifice for them and they see their daddy. My children look to me for love, encouragement, and faith because they see their daddy. My children model my life because they are my children. None of the aforementioned were factual for how my children looked at me when they were birthed. It took time for associations to be made. It took faithfulness on my part to show them the goodness of a father. Today, nobody could ever tell them they belong to someone else. Their absolute faith is in the fact that I am their father, and nobody can take that away. Any mistaken identity would quickly be corrected. They wear my likeness, share my character, and know my love; they are my children.

The Devil's will is to keep you from recognizing your daddy God as the good father. The Devil's will is to keep you believing you are not legitimate children because you don't look like Him, sharing His character and love. If the Devil can kill your bloodline to Heaven, he has successfully taken faith away, and with it, every promise and provision accessed through faith. The Devil's will is to take your shield away so His lies might prevail against you.

Faith extinguishes every fiery arrow the Devil sends your way. It is our shield against his attacks. We have already established the enemy is disarmed. Daniel 7 tells us of the enemy as a boasting horn. This horn is covered in blasphemy and it will '*defy the Most High and oppress the holy people of the Most High. He will try to change their sacred festivals and laws, and they will be placed under his control for a time, times, and half a time. But then the court will pass judgment, and all his power will be taken away and completely destroyed.*' Daniel 7:25-26.

The enemy has a big dirty mouth. But the blasphemy and boasting of the enemy eventually becomes a major world power. This is the Devil and his will. The Devil uses his blasphemous mouth like a horn to cast lies into the world and build his kingdom. See the enemy wont eradicate the faith of Gods Holy people; but rather, the enemy will attempt to change everything, so that it no longer is authentic or Gods design. The trumpets of the Devil are songs of his will being sung over Gods holy people. Fair is your defense and your offense against the Devil.

Adolf Hitler used his charismatic stage presence to convince people to overthrow a government and commit massive genocide. Most people started off meaning well too. The things Hitler would say sounded great to the people. People adored his persona, and therefore people followed him into great evil. What started with eloquent passion ended in violent oppression? We must be careful not to simply listen to the most eloquent men, those that sound passionate. We must hold everything accountable to the whole Word of God. We must test the Spirits. We must not become faithless followers of men.

The German Gun regulation of the Third Reich passed November 10 1938 loosened gun regulations for Germans. The day after these amazing and freeing laws were passed another law was passed prohibiting all Jews from any form of weaponry or ammunition. The Devil uses this tactic as well. The ultimate goal is to disarm Gods people under the guise of liberty for all. The Devil wants to turn the tables. As it stands, the Devil is the one who has regulations placed against him. Those that believe are supposed to obliterate the Devil as they exercise their God given rights. The Devil's will is to disarm and destroy us in the same way he has been disarmed and defeated. The Devil knows faith gives us access to every force of heaven against him and it makes him shudder.

Hebrews 11:1-3 *'Now faith is the substance of things hoped for, the evidence of things not seen. 2 For by it the elders obtained a good testimony. 3 By faith we understand that the worlds were framed by the word of God, so that the things which are seen were not made of the things which are visible.'*

Faith speaks things that are not as if they are, so that they will become.

How does faith defend us? We battle in heavenly realms.

'Put on the full armor of God so that you can take your stand against the Devil's schemes.
12 For our struggle is not against flesh and blood, but against the rulers, against the authorities, against the powers of this dark world and against the spiritual forces of evil in the heavenly realms.' - Ephesians 6:11-12

Faith closes the distance. Arrows are the long-range offense. When I read Ephesians 6, looking at the equipping. The Devil only has one offense described. The flaming arrows of hellish accusation. There isn't anything about the breastplate of righteousness to absorb the impact of close quarters combat. When we close the distance, we become the offense against the enemy. Remember the Devil has been stripped of all authority. Matthew 28:18 has Jesus first words to his disciples as such *"I have been given all authority in heaven and on earth."* Colossians 2:14-15 continues to declare the same truth *"Having canceled the debts ascribed to us in the decrees that stood against us. He took it away. Nailing it to the cross. And having disarmed the rulers and authorities, He made a public spectacle of them, triumphing over them by the cross."* The enemy is left with little more than a trumpet and a voice. From a distance he hurls insults, blasphemes and great boasts. Up close, talk is cheap. The Devil's will is to keep you at a distance. He wants to pierce your heart with lies so you never come close enough to demonstrate that he is already a defeated foe.

Faith speaks things that are not, as if they are, so that they will become. The enemy states things as they seem, so you will believe him and empower the liar. If faith speaks things that are not, as if they are, so that they will become; we must apply this to the truth about identity. I have to agree with God with the faith He has given me about everything He calls me. Here are just a few truths about who we are in Christ.

I am a child of God:

John 1:12 *Yet to all who did receive him, to those who believed in his name, he gave the right to become children of God*

I am adopted through Christ for His pleasure:

Ephesians 1:5 *He predestined us for adoption to sonship through Jesus Christ, in accordance with his pleasure and will*

I am accepted and accepting:

Romans 15:7 *Accept one another, then, just as Christ accepted you, in order to bring praise to God.*

The fullness of Christ dwells in me:

Colossians 2:9-10 *For in Christ all the fullness of the Deity lives in bodily form, 10and in Christ you have been brought to fullness. He is the head over every power and authority.*

I am not a slave to sin:

Romans 6:6 *For we know that our old self was crucified with him so that the body ruled by sin might be done away with, that we should no longer be slaves to sin*

I am chosen, special, royal, and more:

1 Peter 2:9 *But you are a chosen people, a royal priesthood, a holy nation, God's special possession, that you may declare the praises of him who called you out of darkness into his wonderful light.*

I belong to God as the tabernacle of the Holy Spirit:

1 Corinthians 6:19-20 *Do you not know that your bodies are temples of the Holy Spirit, who is in you, whom you have received from God? You are not your own; 20 you were bought at a price. Therefore honor God with your bodies.*

I am already raised with Christ in heavenly places:

Colossians 3:1-3 *Since, then, you have been raised with Christ, set your hearts on things above, where Christ is, seated at the right hand of God. 2 Set your minds on things above, not on earthly things. 3 For you died, and your life is now hidden with Christ in God.*

I am new:

2 Corinthians 5:17 *"Therefore, if anyone is in Christ, he is a new creation; old things have passed away; behold, all things have become new."*

My sonship is through faith:

Galatians 3:26 *"So in Christ Jesus you are all children of God through faith"*

All of these amazing verses have one hook. They require faith. The enemy wishes to keep you as a faithless 'realist' and never entering into these great promises. Galatians 3:26 says sonship is through faith. Look at the context further.

Galatians 3:23-28, *Before the way of faith in Christ was available to us, we were placed under guard by the law. We were kept in protective custody, so to speak, until the way of faith was revealed.*

24 Let me put it another way. The law was our guardian until Christ came; it protected us until we could be made right with God through faith. 25 And now that the way of faith has come, we no longer need the law as our guardian.

26 For you are all children of God through faith in Christ Jesus. 27 And all who have been united with Christ in baptism have put on Christ, like putting on new clothes. 28 There is no longer Jew or Gentile, slave or free, male and female. For you are all one in Christ Jesus.

Everyone born on this planet is made in the image of God, however the path to adoption as sons and daughters is made through faith in Jesus alone. The Devil's will is to get you believe in any other path but faith. The Devil wants the seeker to trust in laws, rules, regulations, restrictions, religion, and good deeds to earn a place with God. The Devil's will is also wants to convince those who are easily complacent to believe that everyone is automatically a child and has a place with God in heaven forever. The Devil's will is for us to have a case of mistaken identity. To be told that just because we are in Gods likeness we are His. It isn't any more true than that I claim someone else's child because it looks a little bit like me. That is called kidnapping, not fatherhood.

Being made in Gods image doesn't automatically make us His child; we must apply all the faith we have in Jesus, the Way, the Truth, and the Life.

-Token Faith

The most foundational source of strength for faith is sonship with God. Apart from Sonship, God doesn't assume responsibility for you any more than you would someone else's kids.

Chuck E Cheese can be a fun place if you have tokens. Is it just me, or do you frequently get asked for tokens by kids you don't know? A few times I've had kids I've never met run up to me and simply ask 'can I have some tokens please?" Tell me, would you oblige? I simply tell them, 'these tokens are for my children, and you... who are you again?' I do this for two reasons, to tell the truth and because it's fun to watch them run off after decline what they want and express interest in the person first. The fact is, I'd love to give them a token in exchange for a brief conversation; but that never happens. More valuable than the token in my hand is the person. I cannot express blessing to those that I don't know and are not willing to know me. This is true for all good gifts for *Every good gift and every perfect gift is from above, and comes down from the Father of lights, with whom there is no variation or shadow of turning.'* James 1:17. I don't become a father because I gave out tokens, I freely give tokens to my kids because they are mine and I am theirs.

Tokens are like faith. A token can be spent on anything in heaven. When you apply faith, you believe it will produce what it was designed to do. God's tokens are only accessible through adoption as a son or daughter. God takes great joy in handing out tokens to His own. God is not so interested in giving tokens to those that don't participate in His family.

You start with one token. This measure of faith is given to all people. The faith token has to be applied to the promise of Jesus for adoption as a son or daughter. The price for adoption was paid by Jesus' precious shed blood. Jesus wouldn't be a good father if He adopted you and didn't take you in immediately. As a legitimate child of God, we can go to Him for more and more faith to face every need.

Hebrews 4:16 *'Let us then with confidence draw near to the throne of grace, that we may receive mercy and find grace to help in time of need.'*

The Devil's will is for us to put faith in our falleness so that even if we return to the Father, we will do so as an indentured servant and not a son. The prodigal son asked for all of his tokens in advance, and then spent them on perishable things in the world. The prodigal spent lots of time pondering this proposal for the good father he abandoned: *"I will set out and go back to my father and say to him: Father, I have sinned against heaven and against you. 19 I am no longer worthy to be called your son; make me like one of your hired servants.'"* Luke 15:18-19. This kind of thinking might be packaged as humility, the Devil's will is to exploit the sorrow of repentance so you never accept your sonship ever again, so you never ask for another token. The Devil was wrong, the Father didn't acknowledge the prodigals offer to work as a servant, the father instantly celebrated, restored, and reinstated the son as a son. God is so good. God isn't interested in your offer, unless that offer is to come home to Him as a son or daughter.

I've spent so much of this time talking about our adoption as sons and daughters to lay a solid foundation for the things of faith. Again I say: the most foundational source of strength for faith is sonship with God. Faith is not earned through religion, regulations, or law. A good Father who knows His children well gives out faith as tokens. There is no access to effective faith outside of the Fathers adoption.

The fiery arrows of the enemy are accusations, blasphemies, and under-qualified boasts. Fight fire with fire. If the enemy makes accusations, faith gives you the authority to shout back at him the truth about salvation and righteousness. If the enemy blasphemes, take them captive and tell the truth of about the greatness of God. If the enemy boasts, boast louder of Christ. You need faith to do all these things.

Faith allows you to brush the accusations of the enemy off, because of the complete covering work of Christ. Faith gives you the audacity to remind the Devil that he is nothing but a crushed snake and a toothless lion. Faith allows you to boast in God, His greatness and power to heal and restore. Faith gives you the ability to take God at His promise and never waver.

Romans 8:28 And we know that God causes everything to work together for the good of those who love God and are called according to his purpose for them.

Keep this in mind; faith does not produce bratty and entitled kids. The Devil's will is for you to believe faith doesn't work because you don't get everything you ask for. The Devil calls Jesus a liar when Jesus says in John 14:14 *'If you ask anything in my name, I will do it.'* The Devil uses this as imperial evidence against Gods promise. The Devil doesn't want you to know the context. Reading the whole context of John 14 you will find out that Jesus isn't saying we should pray selfish prayers, and He will give us a favorable response. Jesus is giving His farewell speech. Jesus is telling them He is going to be with the Father, and to prepare a place for them. Jesus is telling them He will send them the Spirit of Truth. Jesus is commissioning His people to do everything He has commanded. Jesus is confronting the disciple's love and purpose. Jesus is assuring the disciples of His active power and provision among them even after He is gone from them in the flesh. John 14:14 is about asking Jesus to supply the mission, miracle, and ministry according to His command and our fellowship with Him. The 'anything' we ask must be according to the purpose of God being accomplished through you. We cannot put faith in anything that is detached from Gods purpose and expect to remain powerful.

Faith directs Gods power for wholeness. Jesus said to the leper in Luke 17:19 and *'your faith has made you whole.'* Jesus said to the woman with the issue of blood, *'your faith has healed you.'* In Luke 8:48. The word spoken in both cases was 'sozo.' Both cases also were separate from an initial healing. Both the leper and the woman already were healed of what had deemed them unclean upon their initial encounter with Jesus. Yet a second encounter called them whole – 'sozo.' This word 'sozo' was spoken according to their faith. God does the healing, but we apply our faith for wholeness.

Wholeness is so much more than simple healing. The leper and woman were made whole, sozo. This means they were completely restored to whatever they were meant to be – they were justified and made righteous by the faith applied towards Christ. Healing wasn't enough, damage was done by the sickness, and replacement was called for.

The truth about faith is it is required for complete Salvation, Justification, Righteousness, and Wholeness. They are actually a package deal. Salvation is freedom from the mutilation of the enemy, security, and Kingdom resources. Justification is the restoration of the standard. Righteousness is returning to the default for creation, as you should be, as God intends you to be. Sozo wholeness is what happens when all of these are put together. Sozo happens when Jesus rescues you, resources you, heals you, and restores the whole standard. Just as these things come as a whole package, you cannot believe for one and not the others. You cannot believe for salvation and reject righteousness and wholeness. It's the Devil's will to create a disconnect through lies about what any of these are, so that you don't live in any of them.

As I write this, I remember an interaction just this morning. I needed to bring correction to a long time Christian (she is old enough to be my grandmother.) I was just talking about her and she walked into the room. I said 'Speaking of the saint!'
She responded with a flushed face, 'I am most definitely not a saint.'
My response, 'you are a saint saved by grace, not a sinner. Your sin was separated from you as far as the east is from the west, it cannot identify you any longer.'

Remember, we ought not have faith for salvation, yet deny righteousness. The Devil's will is to make salvation less than it is, justification and righteousness unattainable, and wholeness reserved for heaven. The Devil knows if you have faith for all of these, you have no faith for his lies; thus he loses.

Faith can easily be put in the wrong identity. The identity that has your faith, has you. The Devil's will is to see your faith misplaced, so that your whole self too would be misplaced outside of Gods promise, power, and provision.

David killed Goliath with a sling and a stone. I've heard so many messages on David practicing in the field with his shepherd's weapons, throwing his rod and swinging it around. Slinging stones thousands of times preparing to defend sheep from predators. While there may have been some historic evidence, there is very little biblical evidence to substantiate the claims. David used something familiar, that's about all I know for sure. I also know something else for sure – David could have used a fly swatter and still won. Why, because David didn't have faith in his skills, it was all in his God. He said, *'You come against me with sword and spear and javelin, but I come against you in the name of the Lord Almighty, the God of the armies of Israel, whom you have defied. 46 This day the Lord will deliver you into my hands, and I'll strike you down and cut off your head. This very day I will give the carcasses of the Philistine army to the birds and the wild animals, and the whole world will know that there is a God in Israel.'* 1 Samuel 17:45-46. David mentioned Goliaths weapons, but not his own. He said he was coming against Goliath in the name of the Lord Almighty. Then he said he was going to cut Goliaths head off. David used Goliaths sword by the way to accomplish that. Faith says, "I'll use what's in my hand, God will secure the victory." Faith also speaks with such courage that it threatens the enemy with its own weapons. The Devil's will is to use the word of God to condemn you. Faith takes the Word of God and uses it against the Devil to deliver defeat. Revelation 12:11 *And they overcame him by the blood of the Lamb, and by the word of their testimony; and they loved not their lives to the death.* Not only does faith extinguish the enemy's fiery arrows, but also faith redirects every attack to make casualties in the Devil's camp.

The truth about faith is that it turns every weapon of the enemy into an offense for the righteous. Faith must be in Jesus, not our skillsets. Practice faith alone. The Devil's will is to get you to trust your skills, and call them Gods power; but be honest, that's just mans power and it isn't worth comparing.

-Broken Faith and Infomercials.

I actually like watching infomercials. Are you with me? It's fun to watch people demonstrate and sell things I typically wouldn't buy. My favorite are the kitchen gadgets; they make cooking look like a party that I'd love to be invited to. I bought a guitar once off an infomercial. It was created by and stamped with the name of a famous guitarist. I listened to this guitarist play the guitar and I marveled – take my money now! I want it now. I got the guitar and quickly realized, it doesn't sound the same when I play it, and it didn't play very easily either. This guitar was mass manufactured as cheaply as possible then put into the hands of an expert to sell. The expert guitar player could make the cheapest guitar sound good. His skill helped him navigate the guitar with ease where just about anyone else would have issues. I was disappointed, I felt like I had been lied to. My faith in the brand, the musician, and the guitar were completely broken. It's the Devil's will to do the same in our churches. It's the Devil's will to get you to place your faith in a man, a brand 'denomination', or a program. They all will fail you. You will feel like you spent yourself and your resources on a sham. If your faith is placed in your pastor, denomination, or programming; no matter how amazing, you'll feel lied to and eventually scammed into bringing your tithe to fuel another corporate monster. Going to church shouldn't feel like watching the best infomercial you've ever watched and then feeling disappointed when the faith you bought into doesn't work. It's the Devil's will to discourage your faith by discrediting your church.

I've had the conversation so many times. People find out I'm a pastor and then they tell me why they don't go to church. 'I used to go all the time, then the pastor had an affair or 'input any moral failure' and I realized that the man of God I was following was just an imposter.' The faith in the church is quickly left just as broken as the man who was leading it. The Devil's will is for you to place your faith in the church, leadership, and programming so that when they fail, you never re-associate with the fellowship of the saints. It's the Devil's will to see you ostracized and voluntarily excluded from the body of Christ because of broken and misappropriated faith.

There is this puzzling little occurrence in Mark 9:23-24 '*23 Jesus said to him, "If you can believe, all things are possible to him who believes."*

24 Immediately the father of the child cried out and said with tears, "<u>Lord, I believe; help my unbelief!</u>"

25 When Jesus saw that the people came running together, He rebuked the unclean spirit, saying to it, "Deaf and dumb spirit, I command you, come out of him and enter him no more!"

What is it then? Is there faith in Jesus or not? 'I believe; help my unbelief.' Puzzling isn't it. Look at the words original meanings. To believe is to have confidence in what you know to be absolutely true. The word used for unbelief points to two things: the wanting for belief, and the withholding of belief in divine power. The man believed in Jesus, but he was withholding belief for the major miracle. The man was admitting that he had want for faith in an area where faith was misappropriated and withheld. The man had a son possessed of a demon. The Spirit would cause the child to harm himself, lose his senses and convulse. The father was saying essentially; 'I believe in you Jesus, I just need help in replacing misplaced faith.' It was traditionally understood in his day that spiritual oppression was repercussion for sin. The idea was that God wouldn't undo the oppression, as it was a punishment for something. The 'unbelief' was belief in the wrong doctrine. The man was acknowledging the desire for something greater, and acknowledging his failure to put faith in the right things. It's possible to believe in Jesus, but not for wholeness. If this is you, you're the one who says 'I believe, help my unbelief.' It's the Devil's will to justify your unbelief with lies, so that you never live in victory over his oppression. You have to acknowledge misappropriated or broken faith to see a greater measure of functional faith in Christ.

Every attempt to explain why you or anyone else who is in Christ is not 'sozo' whole is a demonstration of unbelief. The Devil's will is for you to keep demonstrating unbelief so that you never demonstrate faith.

-Here's My Debit Card!

Sometimes I do something very dangerous. I give my 12-year-old daughter my debit card; usually with very clear direction. Never once has she looked back at me and asked, 'Are you sure there's enough money in your bank account?' She just said thanks and ran off to accomplish what she intended to do with that card. Faith kind of looks like that. God puts his card in our hand, a signet ring on our finger. The signet ring is special. It gave full purchasing power to the one who wears it on the behalf of the family.

Sometimes my children are too honoring, too frugal; I wonder where they get it. We were at an ice cream parlor with friends. I reached into my wallet and grabbed a twenty-dollar bill. I sent my two children to the line and instructed them to purchase whatever they desire. They came back with one large ice cream to share and 14 dollars change. Who does that? My response was 'thanks for bringing all this change back, but I did say you could have anything you wanted. Why only one ice cream, one topping and two spoons?'

'You said we could get what we want, you didn't tell us to spend all the money.'

My children got what they wanted; they wanted to share an experience together. My children didn't pocket the change; my children didn't exploit my kindness and 'riches' for their benefit. My children used my resources to get what they wanted and nothing more. This is faith as it should be. I put faith in my children when I gave them the money, believing it was more than enough. Seeing they had more than enough, they didn't have a poverty mindset about the abundance; my children choose what they wanted and were satisfied.

1 Timothy 6:6-10 *Yet true godliness with contentment is itself great wealth. ₇ After all, we brought nothing with us when we came into the world, and we can't take anything with us when we leave it. ₈ So if we have enough food and clothing, let us be content.*

₉ But people who long to be rich fall into temptation and are trapped by many foolish and harmful desires that plunge them into ruin and destruction. ₁₀ For the love of money is the root of all kinds of evil. And some people, craving money, have wandered from the true faith and pierced themselves with many sorrows.

Faith is not to be abused for personal riches. God desires for us to be content with the basics of life, so that we can have more to spend on the true purpose of our life; to see His Kingdom expand on earth as it is in heaven. Faith does something special to us; it causes generosity to fill our lives.

Faith and generosity go hand and hand. We need more faith for generosity than prosperity. The Devil's will is for you to believe the lie that your faith is better placed for prosperity than generosity. It takes incredible faith in first world America to stop making prosperity the goal of our lives, and start seeing generosity as the motive for every increase.

2 Corinthians 9:6-8 Remember this: Whoever sows sparingly will also reap sparingly, and whoever sows generously will also reap generously. ₇Each one should give what he has decided in his heart to give, not out of regret or compulsion. For God loves a cheerful giver. ₈And God is able to make all grace abound to you, so that in all things, at all times, having all that you need, you will abound in every good work

Generosity is not giving what's left over at the end of the week. Generosity is intentional faith. We need faith to share the main portion, you won't starve, and on the contrary, you will be filled. Proverbs 11:25 A generous soul will prosper, and he who refreshes others will himself be refreshed. Faith tells us that God will supply our every need. God won't let us die in poverty as a result of generosity. The Devil's will is to get you to believe the lie that the bank account dictates your capacity to be generous. Faith tells you that you're holding God's debit card and God's commission to see the resources of heaven expand through the whole earth. The question is, what are you doing with Gods debit card? Two more scriptures and I'll leave this alone, sorry, not sorry.

1 Chronicles 29:11-12 *Yours, O LORD, is the greatness and the power and the glory and the splendor and the majesty, for everything in heaven and on earth belongs to You. Yours, O LORD, is the kingdom, and You are exalted as head over all. 12Both riches and honor come from You, and You are the ruler over all. Power and might are in Your hand, and it is in Your hand to exalt and to give strength to all.*

Matthew 6:24-25 *No one can serve two masters: Either he will hate the one and love the other, or he will be devoted to the one and despise the other. You cannot serve both God and money. 25Therefore I tell you, do not worry about your life, what you will eat or drink; or about your body, what you will wear. Is not life more than food, and the body more than clothes?*

The Devil's will is to confuse what to have faith for. Faith for prosperity rather than generosity and provision is a great lie. Our faith is for the manifestation of Heaven on earth, not the establishment of our own little fiefdoms. Remember Jesus is Lord; there is no rule, reign, or ownership other than His for the believer.

Faith has its origin in sonship with God. As adopted children and joint heirs our faith does not have its origin in religion, but our relation to the Father of lights from whom every good gift comes. Faith flows from an identity that has been set free from sin, made as we should be, and no longer rooted in falleness. Faith Speaks to the lies and accusations of the enemy with truth and confidence, nullifying the Devil's attack. Faith is required for Salvation, Justification, Righteousness, and Wholeness. Faith is the active agent in seeing the Kingdom of Heaven on Earth as it is in heaven. The Devil's will is to prevent you from seeing the Kingdom on Earth by misdirecting faith towards sin, man, and money. There is nothing supernatural about sin, man, or money – therefore the Devil's will is to nullify your faith. 'Faith is confidence in what we hope for and assurance about what we do not see.' Hebrews 11:1. It is the Devil's will to fix you on past failures, and make you sure of only what you can see and control. The Devil's will is to nullify faith and replace it with religion and control.

LOVE SICK

I am going to talk about Love. I am going to talk about sex. I am going to talk about sexuality. But above all of these things, I am going to talk about Jesus. Jesus is love. It's the Devil's will to confuse everything about love, so that love becomes everything but love.

The talk goes something like this, "When two people love each other very much…" and in so many words: When people love each other they have sex and make children. We do our very best to navigate the discomfort, but it's usually awkward for everyone involved. Is it possible from an early age, we teach sex wrong? In the 'talk' we essentially say that the greatest expression of love is sex. This is ingrained in their minds and sex becomes the ultimate expression of loving another person. We not only give our children longings to love deeply, but we give them an unhealthy view of love. Sex is incredibly satisfying, but Love is incredibly sacrificial. Sex and Love are not the same thing. Both are gifts from God, and it's the Devil's will to confuse Gods intention with false definition.

I came out swinging. If there is one chapter I really don't want to be misinterpreted in, this is it. Love is what God says it is, not what we define it as. In an effort to redefine love, we attempt to redefine love – God is love, God defines Himself, God defines love – not us. Love outside of Gods ordination is not love at all.

-Love Sick

Sickness tests your capacity for love. We had friends visiting from out of state with their baby. The sickness took its turns on all of us. It was a relay race of emptying the contents of our stomachs and bowels for 18 hours each. We laughed a lot about it. We shared in sickness. We shared in support of each other. Getting water and crackers. Providing space for rest and laughter as good medicine. I can't look at that visit any other way. We had lots of fun planned for our time with our friends; but I couldn't have felt more loved, more intimate with my friends and family during that hellish 4 days. We were embraced in our sickness, not rejected. The fear of catching the sickness was an after thought next to the need to be there providing every need including the good medicine of joy and laughter through community. It's the Devil's will to make the sacrifice of love unappealing compared to the services it might provide for you. Sharing love is shared sacrifice. Jesus modeled the sacrifice of love in its greatest measure. *Greater love has no one than this: to lay down one's life for one's friends.* –John 15:13.

So many of us are sick and in need of love. The sickness called lovelessness produces these symptoms: Impatience, Unkindness, Jealousy, Boastfulness, Pride, Self-seeking, Irritability, Anger, Unforgiveness, Giving up, Hopelessness, Faithlessness, and Wrath. Do any of these things feel familiar to you? Do you struggle with any of these things? You're not alone, you need real love. If I were to equate sex as the greatest expression of love, I would expect every symptom of the aforementioned sickness to go away when I experience sexual release. The fact is they don't go away because love does not find its greatest expression outside of sacrifice, and the greatest love is sacrifice unto death.

John 13:35 *By this everyone will know that you are my disciples, if you love one another.*

Again, if love finds it's greatest expression through sex, why isn't church just a big orgy. Close the book in offense and let the Devil win if you want. This is the truth. How we love one another is found when the fellowship of saints surrounds each other with an attitude to treat the symptoms of the loveless sickness with love itself. A loving community makes the exchange. Surrounding one another in prayer we help one another deal with every symptom of lovelessness. We gently and lovingly approach the symptoms with the truth. I am not loving my brother in the Lord if I allow him to hold on to unforgiveness any more than if I let them barf their guts out while I hold the cure in my hands.

The worst sickness I remember being through was severe dehydration. I had a 12-hour marathon of a very physical game with my students back when I was a youth pastor. The nature of the game only gave breaks when you were 'out.' However in my classic competitive nature, I took very few breaks and when I did, coffee was my choice drink. I needed the caffeine to keep going into the early morning hours after a long night of competition. Exhausted I slept for ten hours as soon as I got home. I woke up feeling horrible. I couldn't keep anything down. I was so weak I needed my tiny wife to help me to the bathroom; she loved me so much. She prayed over me, she supplied every need. She provided peace and rest. She did everything a good wife does for a sick husband. As soon as we learned the issue was dehydration, love took another form. I wasn't allowed to turn down water because it just came back up. She made me drink a concoction of salty and sugary water she found online to replace lost electrolytes. She didn't care if I liked the taste, she cared that I got well. Love took action when there was a clear diagnosis and solution. Love no longer accepted me as I was in hope I would get better on my own. Love stepped in with the solution and cast all else aside.

Acceptance is not love. Acceptance says, 'I know you're sick, but I am okay with you staying sick.' My wife accepted me, but not my sickness. Love works that way. Because we love people, we cannot accept their symptoms of lovelessness. The symptoms of lovelessness again are: Impatience, Unkindness, Jealousy, Boastfulness, Pride, Self-seeking, Irritability, Anger, Unforgiveness, Giving up, Hopelessness, Faithlessness, and Wrath. All of these things are unacceptable in the context of love. Treat them as you would any sickness, with the antidote, Love.

Here's the antidote: *Love is patient and kind. Love is not jealous or boastful or proud ₅ or rude. It does not demand its own way. It is not irritable, and it keeps no record of being wronged. ₆ It does not rejoice about injustice but rejoices whenever the truth wins out. ₇ Love never gives up, never loses faith, is always hopeful, and endures through every circumstance.* – 1 Corinthians 13:4-7

Every attribute of love can be applied to treat lovelessness. Every attribute of love, even love itself has its source in Jesus for God is love. If a person is suffering from lovelessness the antidote is in Jesus and the hands of those who are loved by Him.

-Why Me?

I am going to push back on a traditionally accepted phrase. 'You can't love others until you first love yourself.' Usually people applaud this, call it wisdom and move on with their obsession with self-love. This is the Lion Kings approach. The king of the pride is the Alpha male. The alpha doesn't do very much hunting, but when the rest of the pride makes a kill, the alpha feasts first. The king fills his belly as full as it can be. The king growls and swats at the rest of the pride if they approach for a portion. Nobody gets a portion unless the king is full. This is what loving out of the 'me first' mentality looks like. Even more sadly, we are completely incapable of providing enough love for ourselves. There is little to nothing for leftovers. We will perpetually be love starved, and our lives will be growls and swats at those who seek to have a portion of your self-love. Love starved people turn to counterfeits to fill the void. Sex, and masturbation top the list. The symptoms of lovelessness get louder, the hunger grows and satisfaction, even for a moment becomes the longing of every heart. This is not a life of love.

The most common scripture the Devil wills to use to justify the 'love yourself first' movement are the greatest commands clarified by Jesus in Mark 12:30-31 *Love the Lord your God with all your heart and with all your soul and with all your mind and with all your strength.' 31The second is this: 'Love your neighbor as yourself.' No other commandment is greater than these."* How can you love your neighbor if you don't love yourself? The question isn't if you love yourself. It's why. If we can correct why we love ourselves, we can change the world.

1 John 4:7-8 *Beloved, let us love one another, because love comes from God. Everyone who loves has been born of God and knows God. 8Whoever does not love does not know God, because God is love.*

Love has its origin in God. Jesus' love is the source of all love. Loving me is not my job. Loving me is Gods job and nobody can do it like He does. I love me, not out of a love void. I don't need any more love than I already have in Jesus. Jesus love is infinite and complete love. There is no lack; there is no lovelessness in Christ. I love me because He loves me. I love me because I love the things He loves. I love my neighbor because I love the people He loves. Don't get it twisted. Loving me is a completed job. I simply love what God loves, I love my neighbor as I love myself, for the same reasons too. Jesus loves me, and He loves them too. It's the Devil's will to persuade us that Gods love isn't enough. It's the Devil's will to turn us into loveless, sick, and unsatisfied people with a good excuse not to love fully. If you know God, you know His love. If you know His love, you give it freely out of His abundance.

One more pushback using scripture: 2 Timothy 3:1-7
But mark this: There will be terrible times in the last days. 2 People will be lovers of themselves, lovers of money, boastful, proud, abusive, disobedient to their parents, ungrateful, unholy, 3 without love, unforgiving, slanderous, without self-control, brutal, not lovers of the good, 4 treacherous, rash, conceited, lovers of pleasure rather than lovers of God— 5 having a form of godliness but denying its power. Have nothing to do with such people.
6 They are the kind who worm their way into homes and gain control over gullible women, who are loaded down with sins and are swayed by all kinds of evil desires, 7 always learning but never able to come to a knowledge of the truth.

I see the list of discriptives in 2 Timothy 3 starting with 'people will be lovers of themselves.' This is not a good thing. I see the list in somewhat of a progression. Self-love is the gateway to every other travesty mentioned. It is the Devil's will to open the door to lovelessness by focusing you on yourself.

Loving myself is not my job, neither is hating myself. People are such extremists sometimes. Remember we love ourselves because Jesus loves us. We take care of and love that which He loves. We don't love ourselves based on our own merit. *We love only because He first loved us.* 1 John 4:19. Not only is loving me not my job, but I am incapable of love unless I let God love me completely. I have not accepted the love of God if I continue to hate myself. Consider the kind of relationships we would have if we hated the things the people we care about love. Would you ever agree on anything? I must love me, but I do it for the same reason God loves me. The Devil's will is for you to hate people by seeing yourself as hated by God. If you are identifying as a sinner, you cannot be loved, you are only defiled and corrupted. Titus 1:15 *To the pure, all things are pure, but to those who are corrupted and do not believe, nothing is pure. In fact, both their minds and consciences are corrupted.* If you allow yourself to be defined as a sinner, you will not know the Love completely. Love purifies. I cannot hate myself because of what should have been purified. To the degree you identify with your own corruption, you will struggle to know Love.

Psalm 6:16-19

There are six things the Lord hates,
   seven that are detestable to him:
17   haughty eyes,
      a lying tongue,
      hands that shed innocent blood,
18   a heart that devises wicked schemes,
      feet that are quick to rush into evil,
19   a false witness who pours out lies
      and a person who stirs up conflict in the community.

We are allowed to hate the old self. We are allowed to hate the decisions the old self makes. We are not allowed to hate the new self. 2 Corinthians 5:16-18. *So from now on we regard no one according to the flesh. Although we once regarded Christ in this way, we do so no longer. 17Therefore if anyone is in Christ, he is a new creation. The old has passed away. Behold, the new has come! 18All this is from God, who reconciled us to Himself through Christ and gave us the ministry of reconciliation*

Jesus loved me out of sin and into newness; righteousness is newness; (righteous is the one who is as he should be.) I am no longer allowed to regard myself as the man I was, I can love the new creation while hating what is passed away. I laid the old man down with Christ in the waters of baptism.

Romans 6:5-11

For if we have been united together in the likeness of His death, certainly we also shall be in the likeness of His resurrection, 6 knowing this, that our old man was crucified with Him, that the body of sin might be done away with, that we should no longer be slaves of sin. 7 For he who has died has been freed from sin. 8 Now if we died with Christ, we believe that we shall also live with Him, 9 knowing that Christ, having been raised from the dead, dies no more. Death no longer has dominion over Him. 10 For the death that He died, He died to sin once for all; but the life that He lives, He lives to God. 11 Likewise you also, reckon yourselves to be dead indeed to sin, but alive to God in Christ Jesus our Lord.

We must consider ourselves dead to sin and alive in Christ. This is how we rectify the 'love hate' relationship with ourselves. The things we hate are dead and gone, what's worth loving is alive and well in Christ.

-Love is Love

This is the sex part. You might not agree with me on everything I say. I ask you not to agree with me, agree with God and His Word.

In an effort to redefine love, we attempt to redefine God. God is love; to redefine love is to redefine God. But *'Jesus Christ is the same yesterday, today, and forever.'*

Hebrews 13:8. If Jesus is the same, Love is the same. Love doesn't change with the times. Love is as eternal and unchangeable as God Himself. Not only is God completely beyond definition, He is way beyond re-definition.

The Devil's will is to confuse love with sexual attraction so that love loses its primary demonstration in sacrifice, replacing it with personal gratification. The moment sexual attraction takes over, we become self-seeking. The goal is a personal and intimate experience for oneself. Again, the greatest expression of love is not sex; it's sacrifice unto death. I don't pick the person I will love for the rest of my life based on sexual attraction. While I find my wife sexually attractive, I found the one I could give my life to without getting anything in return. I found the one worth my whole life, every sacrifice, every thing. That's my love. I found the one God pointed out to me and said, 'there's your partner in ministry.' The spiritual attraction led to every other form of affection for my wife. When sexual attraction becomes the driving force in a relationship, the relation is no longer sacrificial or spiritual, it's about what you might get out of it; it's all flesh.

The object of our love must be according to the design God has for us. God designed each of us for good works according to His purposes. There are a few constants for every believer. The first command God made to man is in Genesis 1:27-28 is one of these constants.

So God created man in His own image; in the image of God He created him; male and female He created them. 28God blessed them and said to them, "Be fruitful and multiply, and fill the earth and subdue it; rule over the fish of the sea and the birds of the air and every creature that crawls upon the earth."

Man was made in the image of God for the purpose of God, to fill the earth through multiplication and to establish complete dominance on earth under the design of the Kingdom of Heaven. Primary to the existence of every person is the command to multiply. The world might call many combinations of relationship love, but only one combination fits into the plan for multiplication. The plan for multiplication is reserved for a covenant bound family.

I personally know someone who once saw their purpose in life to be to create as many progeny as they can. Their reason: their DNA is a gift to the world. Sounds crazy huh. However they are only partly right. They are supposed to multiply within covenant relationship with one woman, not just any woman. This person saw it as civil responsibility to sow his seed wherever he pleased while failing to see the responsibility to love the field he planted in. If you sow good seed, but don't tend the field, weeds will take over every time. Do not justify sex outside of a covenant marriage as fulfilling Gods purposes; it's only the Devil's will for you to do so.

It is wrong to call sexual attraction love. If God is Love, does this mean He is sexually attracted to us? Yuck! Jesus was born of a virgin y'all. God places Himself in us by His spirit without sex. Jesus didn't have a wife or children. He was pure through and through. Jesus loved everyone He encountered without sexual ambition. Jesus never loved people because of what He might get out of it. Jesus loved because that's what He does. We need to learn to love as He loves so that we can put sex back in its place as a role reserved for a man and a woman in covenant relationship.

At this point you might be assuming I am getting ready to throw more fodder to the homo-phobic. I'm not. Remember Love isn't afraid of catching anything; love just loves in the right direction. What I am saying is this: God designed you to love the opposite sex. There are only two sexes, male and female. God created both male and female in His image. The bible explicitly says this much. A man plus a woman equals a whole pair. What I am saying is that choosing homosexuality is like settling for two left feet when you could be dancing with one of each. Gods design works for a man and a woman through covenant relationship. It's just the way it was designed. I love all people enough to want to see them live in victory over every deception the Devil wills for me to accept. But while I am at it, let me say this, all sexual immorality is the same to God and it is all sin. Remember sin means you missed the mark. All sexual sin falls short of Gods purpose for sex. All sex outside of the marriage bed of a man and a woman falls short of Gods intended purpose. The purpose finds it's outworking in the multiplication of a household that is submitted to the Kingdom and covered in the love of God. Pay close attention; it isn't God's will for two men to have intercourse than for one man to have it with himself. Let that sink in for a minute. Sexual immorality in every form falls short of its intended and righteous purpose.

-Pornography is Adultery
Song of Solomon 8:4 *"Do not arouse or awaken love until it so desires."* We should not be encouraging children to explore sexual pleasure. There is no turning back.

We live in a day that schools are saying that this is an okay thing to explore at an early age. A Washington post article entitled, "California is Overhauling Sex Education Guidance For Schools — and Religious Conservatives Don't Like It" gives an overall view of the curriculum passed as of Jan. 2016 in the California Health Education Framework. *"In* *kindergarten through third grade, children will learn about gender identity; they'll be taught about <u>masturbation</u> in fourth through sixth grades; in seventh and eighth grade they'll learn about consent and sexual abuse, and in ninth through 12th grade, they'll learn more about "contraception and healthy sexual relationships, including advice for LGBTQ students."*

It is the Devil's will to awaken sexual desire in children at an early age. By encouraging children to explore themselves, and with others sexually, they associate sex with self-pleasure and not an eternal and beautiful expression according to God's purposes. I repeat, it is the Devil's will for a child to see sex and love as something entirely bent to their own desires.

Sleeping men are not curious. The Devil's will is to awaken sexual passion and with it curiosity without a healthy outlet. Children explore sexuality at an early age and then are prohibited from sexual expression with one another. After all we have to draw the line somewhere. The world we live in says children should 'play with themselves by themselves.' The line is drawn when they experiment on each other, and that line is becoming increasingly blurry. A child with no sexual outlet, curiosity, and the Internet will quickly be exposed to the most twisted expressions of sex. The solution is not to allow kids to experiment with each other; the solution is to teach sex as God intends it from an early age. If a sexual appetite is developed at a young age, it will most definitely lead to pornography.

Porneia is the Greek word used for 'Fornication' in the bible. All forms of sexual immorality fall under the of porneia, specifically, adultery, homosexuality, and prostitution. Pornography gets its name from what it is. To participate in the consumption of pornography is likened to all sexual immorality. The one who is addicted to porn is no different from the homosexual or the adulterer, all are committing the same sin, and none are healthy parts of Gods design for sexuality.

Nobody is excluded from the struggle with pornography. Here are a few statistics about pastors from the Barna group cited in their study called 'The Porn Phenomenon.'
-Overall, 21% of youth pastors and 14% of pastors admit they currently struggle with using porn.
-About 12% of youth pastors and 5% of pastors say they are addicted to porn
-87% of pastors who use porn feel a great sense of shame about it.
-55% of pastors who use porn say they live in constant fear of being discovered.

Teens talk about porn as if it isn't an issue: again quoting Barna "When they talk about porn with friends, 89% of teens, and 95% of young adults say they do so in a neutral, accepting, or encouraging way. That is, only one in 20 young adults and one in 10 teens say their friends think viewing pornography is a bad thing."

Lastly comes the scary statistic: One in Three Americans actively seek out pornography at least monthly.

Pornography finds its root in our deepest longing. Love. Love is what we were created for. But when love finds its greatest expression in sex and self-gratification, the Devil's will is present and prevailing. Love and sex must be put back into their proper places as God designed them to be.

When sex can be whatever you want it to be, and sex becomes the ultimate expression of love; love becomes whatever you want it to be. The Devil's will is to make you sick with lovelessness by feeding you fornication and acceptance and calling it love. Love is Love; Love is what God says it is and nothing else. You were created for love, the Devil wishes to confuse love so that he might keep you from fulfilling the most basic of purposes in your life.

-The evidence of love

I drink coffee and tea a lot. As I write this I am sitting down at our churches missional outreach called Royal-tea, and I drink for free. Needless to say, I drink a lot of tea and coffee. I am a bit of a purist though. A few years ago I had an encounter with a Barista at a well-known chain that went as such:

I could never forget her response. The look of disgust. The distain she felt as her bottom lip curled into the pockets of her cheeks when I ordered my drink of choice. "I'd like a quad please."

"Would you like that skim, 2%, whole, or soy?"

"None of them. I'm not ordering a latte. I just want a quad, that's all."

"Wait, you want four shots of espresso all by themselves." The confusion in her eyes seemed to say, "Who would do such a thing?"

"Yes, Straight up please!" My pride grew 3 sizes because I knew what was coming next – The "You must be a real man to drink it like that" statement. - But I was wrong. This barista was different. Her disapproval burned through my confidence and produced a dumbfounded expression as my eyes fell to the countertop.
So I asked her, "Well, then what do you get when you

order?"

"A Chai tea latte, and if I am tired, I'll get it dirty. But only if I need it."

Now, that's not a bad drink. But it isn't coffee. It's tea and steamed milk. And only under the right circumstances might she add a tiny bit of coffee to the mix to make it 'dirty.'

One more question: I couldn't help myself, "Do you even like coffee?"
"Not necessarily by itself, and definitely not espresso. I can enjoy a shot or two in a latte with an extra pump to offset it though."

What just happened? Coffee shops sell 'coffee' but not in it's most concentrated and purest forms. It has to be milked and sugared down to be palatable. If you say you love coffee, Drink COFFEE and LOVE IT! If you say you love Jesus, drink deep of His Spirit and let the whole world know. Don't sell Holy Spirit lattes watered down with the sweet things of life.

1 John 4:12-13 *No one has ever seen God; but if we love one another, God lives in us and His love is made complete in us. 13 This is how we know that we live in Him and He in us: He has given us His Spirit.* God is love and all whom God lives in has complete love. This complete love is

evidenced by one thing alone. He has given us His Spirit. Where God is, Love is. Where Love is, His Spirit is. 2 Corinthians 3:17-18 *Now the Lord is the Spirit, and where the Spirit of the Lord is, there is freedom. 18And we, who with unveiled faces all reflect the glory of the Lord, are being transformed into His image with intensifying glory, which comes from the Lord, who is the Spirit.* The Spirit gives freedom and with that freedom transformation into the image of God with intensifying glory. Love does this! Study the life of Jesus and you will see what love looks like under the jurisdiction of the Spirit.

It is impossible to love completely without the manifestation of the Spirit. We are to be known by our love, but it's what love does that is supernatural. Love breaks sickness, addiction, and casts out demons. Everything the Holy Spirit did through Jesus and His disciples are manifestations of Gods love. Matthew 9:35-38 *Jesus traveled through all the towns and villages of that area, teaching in the synagogues and announcing the Good News about the Kingdom. And he healed every kind of disease and illness. 36 When he saw the crowds, he had compassion on them because they were confused and helpless, like sheep without a shepherd. 37 He said to his disciples, "The harvest is great, but the workers are few. 38 So pray to the Lord who is in charge of the harvest; ask him to send more workers into his fields."*

Love was the motivation behind every healing Jesus performed. Love is supernatural in that it invites the power and Spirit of God to demonstrate His Kingdom. It's the Devil's will to get you to deny the purpose of the miraculous in your daily love life so that you never truly love like Jesus. The evidence that you have love is that you have the Spirit. Let the Spirit be evidenced in your life as God directs the miraculous as the bi-product of His presence and love.

The motive of love is found in contribution not consumption. God is completely self-sustaining, He has no need for love from us, but He loves us so much. God spared nothing, not even His own life in demonstrating His love towards us. The love of God didn't come from a place of need, but supply. God loves because He chooses to share Himself, His image, His Spirit, and His destiny with us. We love because He first loved us. The nature of love is contribution not consumption. Because God has lavished so much love upon us, we have the ability to pour it back out in abundance. We don't love people because we need love; we love people because we have so much love to give.

The love of God supplies every need and fills every void. We cannot love completely while remaining incomplete. This is why we must grab ahold of the wholeness available to us only through Christ. To the degree Christ makes us whole; we can love completely. As we are transformed into His image with intensifying glory, His Spirit increases wholeness and with it the amplitude of love. Love is about contribution from wholeness, not consumption out of lack.

Love is not about mutual contribution. If that were so, God would have demonstrated Love out of some need for love. God is Love, He is infinite, and His love has no limit. God did not create man for reciprocation of love. If God is perfect love, we must apply the model to love itself. Loving for the sake of reciprocation is a dangerous thing. Reciprocation says, 'I scratch your back, and you scratch mine.' Love says, 'let me scratch your back.'

I love my wife very much. Because I love her I do everything I do for her. Because she loves me she does what she does. The vows we took did not say, 'I will love you as long as you love me back.' Our love covenant is not situational. We are committed to love no matter what. When two people are committed to love with or without reciprocation, they are committed to love as God loves. Love contingent on reciprocation is not supernatural love.

Luke 6:32-36 *"If you love those who love you, what credit is that to you? Even sinners love those who love them. 33 And if you do good to those who are good to you, what credit is that to you? Even sinners do that. 34 And if you lend to those from whom you expect repayment, what credit is that to you? Even sinners lend to sinners, expecting to be repaid in full. 35 But love your enemies, do good to them, and lend to them without expecting to get anything back. Then your reward will be great, and you will be children of the Most High, because he is kind to the ungrateful and wicked. 36 Be merciful, just as your Father is merciful."*

Supernatural love loves all people without the need for reciprocation because the love void is completely full, so full love has to overflow. It's the Devil's will to call love something common and natural so that we fail to ever love beyond ourselves. Attempting to love without the fullness of the Spirit is having a form of godliness but denying it's power. The bible says to have nothing to do with those people, so have nothing to do with Love outside of the indwelling of the Spirit of God. It's the Devil's will that your love becomes powerlessly detached from the Spirit and Truth.

IS YOUR BLOWER BLOWING?

Not by might nor by power, but by my Spirit,' says the LORD Almighty.
- Zechariah 4:6
This is how we know that we live in Him and He in us: He has given us His Spirit
- 1 Peter 4:11 *"If anyone speaks, they should do so as one who speaks the very words of God. If anyone serves, they should do so with the strength God provides, so that in all things God may be praised through Jesus Christ. To Him be the glory and the power for ever and ever. Amen.*

I am going to talk about the Holy Spirit, prophecy and healing. You've been warned. There is a divide about these topics, that divide is perhaps one of the Devil's successes. My attempt is for all of us to understand why the divide is the Devil's will to cause persecution from within the church body.

-Furnaces and Radiators

Just as I sat down to write this paragraph 2 things happened. The furnace fan stopped blowing and a lady walked up to me and started a conversation about the Holy Spirit and salvation. I put the furnace aside and started in on the conversation, then another lady joined in and we had a great moment with the Holy Spirit. After this I went to work on the furnace and just as I discovered the issue, the power to the whole city went out. I took a moment to listen to the Lord, not about my problem, but about what He was saying. The blower doesn't have power. My furnace has now become a relatively ineffective radiator.

The heat vents were radiating heat, but they were not efficient, and only effective to have small incremental change on the atmosphere. Jesus is speaking to my heart in this very moment, as I write in a dim room with no power. There is no power to the blower. The gift must be fanned into flame and power must be used to see the effects of the spirit fill rooms and change the atmosphere. The Holy Spirit came like tongues of fire. I look at the furnace and I see the pilot light keeps going without power, there is still supply.

I want to say this as gently as I can, "stop trying to build religion around what gifts must be manifest in order to be verified as spirit filled. If a person is in Christ, He has already sent His Spirit."

The question has now become; does the blower have power? There is a pilot light inside every believer. There is evidence of heat radiating from the life of every believer. If your blower has power, there isn't just evidence in your life, there is evidence in the room when you enter it. Spirit Filled Christians with powered fans change the atmosphere when they walk into a room. The Devil's will is to keep believers from powering their fans by denying the need for a fan. There is much power in numbers. If many Christians gather, the room is changed by the masses. There is no need for a fan, they are all radiators; together they can shift the atmosphere. However, the reality of this powerlessness hits them the moment they leave the gathering. Prayer chains are aimed at mass numbers; gatherings are only effective with many. Individuals walking in great power become a rarity while congregational authority increases. The Devil's will is to discourage the individual from impacting their workplace with the same atmospheric power as the church gathering. The Devil's will is to limit Gods power to the mass gathering. My goal is to help us all acknowledge a greater, environment shifting reality for our daily lives. My objective is to see power sent to your blower motor so that you might transform cities and disciple nations. You were created to be a furnace, not an inefficient radiator.

-Literacy rates and Holy Spirit operation.

I want to acknowledge the Holy Spirit is already deposited in the lives of all those who declare 'Jesus is Lord.' There are many camps of thought that attempt to explain why the Holy Spirit doesn't function the way we witness the Holy Spirit through the life of Jesus and His disciples. The first generations of the church were marked by the miraculous.

Mark 16:17-18
These signs shall follow them that believe; In my name shall they cast out Devil's; they shall speak with new tongues; they shall take up serpents; and if they drink and deadly thing, it shall not hurt them; they shall lay hands on the sick, and they shall recover.

Jesus said it, and then it happened. It kept happening for the first 200 years of church history. Then these things became less common when the Spirit of Truth was exchanged for a linty of religious practices, meeting places, and man guided teaching. The argument against signs wonders and prophecy from the intellectual Christian spectrum is that there is no longer a need for the miraculous because of the completed cannon of the word of God. They call the miraculous a forerunner to something higher:

understanding. They say knowledge has been made known, historically proven through the miraculous, and now stands alone as the unrivaled and only essential evidence of Jesus. There is little to no scriptural support for the idea that the miraculous is no longer needed because the scriptures have been proven and canonized. Of the most popular is this:

1 Corinthians 13:8-10
"Love never fails. But where there are prophecies, they will cease; where there are tongues, they will be stilled; where there is knowledge, it will pass away. 9 for we know in part and we prophesy in part, 10 but when completeness comes, what is in part disappears."

The Devil's will is to utilize scripture, taken out of its context; and placed into the context of His argument. This is evidence of His will being made known from the pulpit of every church that does not teach the Holy Spirit as active and essential in the supernatural outworking of your faith. Love never fails, this is true. But scripture tells us more when you read it together. Scripture tells us Love is impossible without the Spirit. 1 John 4:12-13 *"No one has ever seen God; but if we love one another, God lives in us and His love is made complete in us. 13 This is how we know that we live in Him and He in us: He has given us His Spirit."* The Holy Spirit is not a thing; it is the person of God. If God is there, why would He sacrifice what is natural to Him for what is natural to man? The Holy Spirit is the active agent behind every word of God.

The Trinity is our human way of trying to explain the vastness of God. God is Father, Son, and Holy Spirit. All three are One God. They are not parts of God, but collectively and independently God Himself. An easy way to think of the three operating together is: God the Father is the mouth that speaks, The Son is the Word spoken, and the Spirit is the active power behind the spoken word of God. Just like it is bad parenting to make promises and threats without follow-through. The Holy Spirit is the follow-through for every spoken promise from God.

My eight-year-old son has recently started learning how to write in beautiful cursive letters. He only knows how to write his name and a few other letters. If I were to write him a book using cursive, would he be able to read it? I'd have to wait for him to learn and mature in his knowledge of the style of handwriting before he could ever comprehend my book. Essentially speaking, my son can read, but He is currently overcoming illiteracy towards the cursive form. The Spirit of God is the foundation for understanding the form of the Son, and the intention of the Father.

The Bible itself is not a replacement as the third

person of the trinity. It's the Devil's will to get you to believe that the bible can replace the Holy Spirit as your teacher. The Bible is a prophetic word aimed with conviction towards your soul. *"For the Word of God is alive and active. Sharper than any double-edged sword, it penetrates even to dividing soul and spirit, joints and marrow; it judges the thoughts and attitudes of the heart."* Hebrews 4:12.

Literacy rates in the world are shocking evidence of the tiny world mindsets 1st world teachers are coming from. If it were possible to teach that the only thing we need is the Bible without prophecy, healing, deliverance from demons, and the raising of the dead; we have to look at the rest of the world. 99.2% of adults in 1st world nations can read. About 2% of Americans have intellectual disabilities. This category makes up a vast majority of those who cannot read in 1st world countries. However South and West Asia have literacy rates around 70% and the southern 2/3 of Africa has a 64% literacy rate. After reading these statistics: does it still make sense that literacy must be a prerequisite for the things of God, the power and calling of God for all people? The first world elitist mindset that substitutes 'reading' for 'operating' in the Spirit is far from accurate. The Holy Spirit demonstrates in a moment what a lifetime of learning cannot. The manifestation of the Holy Spirit through the miraculous demonstrates the Grace and Power of

God in a way no scholar could ever truly comprehend or explain. Every attempt to explain why the Holy Spirit isn't alive and active in prophecy or healing is a demonstration of the Devil's will. The Devil's will is to make us a bunch of talking heads, using lots of wise words, but denying their power. Having a form of Godliness but denying it's power. There are no rules that I cannot quote the same scripture twice in a book so here it is again; pay close attention.

2 Timothy 3:1-7

But mark this: There will be terrible times in the last days. 2 People will be lovers of themselves, lovers of money, boastful, proud, abusive, disobedient to their parents, ungrateful, unholy, 3 without love, unforgiving, slanderous, without self-control, brutal, not lovers of the good, 4 treacherous, rash, conceited, lovers of pleasure rather than lovers of God— 5 having a form of godliness but denying its power. Have nothing to do with such people.

6 They are the kind who worm their way into homes and gain control over gullible women, who are loaded down with sins and are swayed by all kinds of evil desires, 7 always learning but never able to come to a knowledge of the truth.

Having a form of godliness but denying its power…. Always learning but never able to come to a knowledge of the truth. The truth is a Spirit, the Holy Spirit. Do not squelch the Spirit by limiting Him to teaching only. Limiting the Holy Spirit as the

Advocate and Illuminator of the Word is like turning on the furnace without the blower fan. It's about to get deep, the Spirit is the wind upon the vocal cords of Gods very voice box. The spirit comes from the depths of God, as God, traveling from His lungs over His will formed by the voice box and mouth. The Spirit proceeds out of the mouth of God, given form by the living Word Jesus. The Spirit reverberates and resounds throughout all of creation as the Word is spoken. And the same Spirit that spoke all things into creation and rose Christ from the dead, now lives in you. The same words Jesus spoke when He said, 'get up and walk,' or 'your faith has made you whole.' The same Spirit, flows from the lungs of those who have received Him, according to the will of God, and the example in Christ for us to do the very same things. We must speak as those using the very words of God. 1 Peter 4:11 *"If anyone speaks, they should do so as one who speaks the very words of God. If anyone serves, they should do so with the strength God provides, so that in all things God may be praised through Jesus Christ. To Him be the glory and the power for ever and ever. Amen.*

It's the Devil's will for us to do things according to our own intellect and strength so that man gets the praise and not God. *Not by might nor by power, but by my Spirit,' says the LORD Almighty.* - Zechariah 4:6 Gods will is to place things in our destiny that are way beyond our capacity. The truth about the Spirit is that you cannot even come close to His destiny without supernatural power from God Himself. The fullness of the Spirit is the blower on your furnace.

-YouTube tricked me.

About three times a year I decide to pull myself together. I decide to put my body back into top working order. Some things just can't wait until New Years resolution season. I am no foreigner to the diet and fitness life; actually it has always been a passion and interest. Life gets busy; I get out of rhythm and find myself bathing my beard and belly in peanut butter and marshmallows at the end of a long day. I look at my actions, I look at myself and I decide to make the necessary changes to my life. The first hurdle is often the biggest, and I am ashamed to say the first hurdle has stopped me in my tracks. The first hurdle is the planning and learning phase. If I am going to get into shape, I have to develop a plan for diet and fitness. Remember, I am interested in both things. This is when YouTube steps in: I watch videos by the people who are where I want to be, and know what I want to know. I want to know how to apply a diet to my lifestyle while learning from others mistakes and not my own. I want a fitness plan that won't bore me to tears leading me to quit. I've lifted enough weights to know I can only do that for about

3 months out of the year before I get bored. I find videos of people doing extraordinary stuff with their bodies. I get excited. I say to myself 'That's it, I'm going to do that!' Then I spend the next week 'studying' the diet and fitness plan. I watch more videos... I read more blogs. Eventually I feel like an expert. The goal is to know enough to lead myself through the process. The issue is I love the learning so much that I never get to the doing. I do so much study on the program that by the time I am done studying, I feel like an expert that's actually done all that stuff. My process of study had me imagining myself doing cool stuff. My process of study was based on what I believed was possible, but it was worthless knowledge without application. But I look no different because of my knowledge. The Holy Spirit is critical to every application of the knowledge of God. The first hurdle is the acquisition of knowledge. Remember having a form of godliness and denying it's power, ever learning but never knowing; this is the common cycle for most of the powerful potentials in life.

Learning is comfortable and safe. I can do it alone, nobody has to see me. I'm accountable to nothing but myself and I'm used to letting myself down. What I don't want to do is make it all public. I don't want to go through the discomfort and pain of growing. I don't want my butt and thighs to scream at me every time I try to sit on the toilet the day after leg day. I want the comfort of telling someone else how to get fit and healthy. I want someone else to go through the uncomfortable stuff at my recommendation. I didn't just describe myself nearly as much as I have described the vast majority of ministry leaders who deny the Holy Spirit and make recommendations like brutal fitness trainers. The issue, many of these teachers know nothing of the Holy Spirit because it's easier to learn, than to know. It's the Devil's will to keep you ever learning and never knowing the Spirit of truth.

YouTube successfully tricked me into laziness. I have a new rule to get over the first hurdle. Acknowledge that you already know enough to get started. It's okay to learn along the way, you just can't let learning get in the way. The thing we all need to acknowledge is that we need complete dependence on the Holy Spirit to do anything He calls us to. When we depend on Holy Spirit, we no longer depend on our preparation, knowledge, might, power, or skill. Just Holy Spirit and obedience to His direction and call. The Devil's will is to keep you from experiencing and operating in the Holy Spirit by keeping you in the experience and operation of man. God wills for all of us to have His Spirit living through us in a way that is so much larger than life. God's will is to be so evident in the life of the believer that they give Him praise through Jesus.

Gods will is that we speak as those using His very words and serve with His strength. The Devil's will is to keep the supernatural limited to what is natural with man; in other words the Devil's will is for us to do nothing that can only result in God alone being praised.

-Almost everything is for sale

If I have time and money, I can buy just about any skill. I can go to any trade school, give them my time and money and come out with a trade. The most popular reason for investing in learning a trade is to then sell your services using that trade. Sometimes this it's a great frustration to me that I cannot 'legally' do certain kinds of work. I need an electrician's license to install a new electrical service. Nobody asks, "Do you know how to do that?" They ask, "Are you certified." The certification speaks to the ability, but ability doesn't equal certification without proper schooling. The truth about most trades is that they existed for a long time before certifications were required. Today education is an expensive path to careers in skilled trades. The church grabbed ahold of this well before building codes existed too.

Education is the path to success. Education has been the key for the success of societies as a whole for thousands of years. The Romans established educational centers open to all people around 400 B.C. They became the greatest super power of the known world very quickly. Education works. The most educated people in ancient Rome were the rock-stars of their day specifically the philosophers. Trades and philosophy became the backbone of the educational system. Then came Jesus and His Holy Spirit to interrupt the program.

John 14, 15, and 16 are worth studying in depth to get the fullness of what I'm about to say. Take a moment, read them through before coming back to this writing. There are some questions that need answers as we go through this amazing teaching Jesus gave His disciples at the last supper. This is His final sermon; He made it all count and we need to treat these words as if He is speaking them directly to us as His disciples before He hands His work over to us.

Allow these questions to guide deeper discovery from John 14-16.

John 14 Questions.
How are the Father and Christ synchronized in word and deed?
Why are they synchronized?
If someone doesn't believe the words, what evidence is left?

What will those who believe in Jesus do?

What will Jesus do for those who believe?

What does loving Jesus look like?

How does obedience to Jesus look for the believer using the context of John 14:11.

What is Jesus asking the Father to give those who keep the command?

What is the world's response to the gift of the Father?

How will we see Jesus?

What is the ultimate realization for those who believe?

Where/with whom do Jesus and the Father make their home?

Whose words is Jesus speaking?

If He is in us, and we are in Him, and the Father in us, whose words do we speak? Whose work? Whose power?

Who will teach you all things?

What does Jesus leave with us?

John 15 Questions

Who must we be attached to in order to bear fruit?

Do a Greek word study on 'Cuts off' for John 15:2 for better understanding. Hint the word is 'airo'

What makes you clean?

Who 'remains' or 'abides' in whom and why?

Can you bear fruit without abiding in Christ and He in you? What's the evidence of abiding/remaining in Him?

What happens to those who choose not to remain or abide?
What shall also accompany the abiding presence?
What do we do with those words?
What is the end result of using His words?
How do you show yourself to be His disciple?
Aside from the person and words of God, what else must we remain in, and remain in us?
How do we remain in His love?
Whose example are we following?
Why must we remain, whose joy is at stake?
What is the command to love?
To whom is the greatest love demonstrated towards?
How do you know you're a friend of God?
Why did Jesus choose you?
What did Jesus appoint you to?
How do you know if you belong to the world?
Should we be accepted by the world?
What do those who hate God reject?
Who will and must testify?
Does this all scare you a little yet?

John 16 questions:
Why did Jesus tell us what He said in John 14-15?
What will those who persecute you think they are doing?
Why do they do those things?
Why is it for our good that Jesus went to the Father?
What is Jesus sending in His place?

What is the active role of the Spirit towards the sinner?

What is the active role of the Spirit towards the righteous?

What is the active judgment the Spirit delivers?

What will guide you into all truth?

What does the Spirit speak?

How is Jesus glorified?

What is the conduit between Jesus and what is known?

Why don't we have to grieve the loss of Jesus?

When the Holy Spirit comes; what can take away your joy?

What must we do in order to receive? Who do we go to?

When you speak to the Father, whom else are you speaking to?

What is the challenge of our faith in this world?

Why have peace? Why take heart?

I seriously hope you didn't just read those questions and attempt to answer them according to your own understanding. I hope you have taken the time to allow the scripture to speak to you the truth. The words I write are not a substitute for the Holy Scriptures; read the bible before you read what I have to say about it.

You need the Holy Spirit. The Holy Spirit speaks

Gods words through you; the Holy Spirit does Gods work through you. Apart from the fullness of the Holy Spirit, you do not speak according to Gods authority, you do not work according to His power, and you do not bear the kind of fruit that will keep you out of the fire. You are worthless, and everything you do and say is of no value to God apart from His Holy Spirit. If you have been attempting to explain why the Holy Spirit is no longer in full operation: you have been talking your way off the vine and into the fire. These were Jesus last words for a good reason. The truth about the Holy Spirit is that the Holy Spirit turns your life into His life. When your life is His life, it looks like Jesus' life. The Devil's will is to keep you weak and human.

-Don't bring a book to a knife fight; bring a sword!

"Go ahead, see if I care!" he said as he paced towards me, steak knives in each hand. The knives seemed to dance violently in his eight year old hands in sync with the curling of the corner of his mouth. My brother was at it again. The art of being a big brother. He was supposed to be doing the dishes, but couldn't resist torturing me. I had a healthy respect for knives when I was seven. Every scream that I would 'tell' on him was deflected by those words, "God ahead, see if I care!" It was at that moment that I realized that I could not threaten the violent intent with the letter of the law. I needed to be equally equipped to face him with courage. In the case of my brother, I had to get comfortable with knives so they no longer scared me. I knew my brother loved me. I wasn't afraid of him, I was afraid of what the knives would do. As a seven year old it made perfect sense. My solution was to say, "Give me one of those then!" It worked. He approached me with both knives, still dancing in his hands, and said "you sure!" He was still trying to creep me out. I called his bluff and he quit torturing me.

The law, rules, regulations, and codes of ethics mean nothing to someone with criminal intent. People don't kill people because guns exist, people don't stab people because it's lawful. People who do these things do them because they have criminal intent. Nobody has ever said; I didn't know it was against the law to shoot people. There is no amount of legislation that could ever stop a man with criminal intent. Let that sink in. Now pacify the feeling of hopelessness with courage. You are hopeless and will continue to be hopeless if you trust the letter of the law, legislation, or the Bible to restrain criminal conduct. The chief criminal is the Devil. *The Devil comes to steal, kill, and destroy* –John 10:10. There is no law that says these things are okay for the Devil act as a thief, murderer, or destroyer. The Devil's will is completely wrought with criminal intent.

The Devil threatens us with spiritual forces in his hands. As long as you are afraid to embrace the fullness of the Holy Spirit, there is no sword in your hand. The sword of the Spirit must be in your hands. Ephesians 6:17 tells us the sword of the Spirit is the word of God. Remember, the word of God is sharper than any two edged sword. The Greek word for 'word' is rhema. The rhema word does not point to text origin. Rhema words are spoken with a voice and definite meaning. The Rhema word is not limited to the Bible. The Rhema word of God is every word that flows from God. Look again at John 15:7 *'But if you remain in me and my words remain in you, you may ask for anything you want, and it will be granted!'* pair it with Jesus' introduction to this teaching in John 14:10 *'Don't you believe that I am in the Father and the Father is in me? The words I speak are not my own, but my Father who lives in me does his work through me.'* The Rhema word is a prophetic sword that gives you the courage to disarm the Devil. Don't bring a book to a knife-fight; bring a sword. Every time you speak as the mouthpiece of the indwelling Holy Spirit, you speak prophetic truth and power. The Devil's will is to keep your word of faith limited to what you've memorized from the past, not what you're hearing in the Spirit right now.

Following the Spirit requires courage. The most referenced greeting from heavens angels is 'fear not' or 'do not be afraid.' When Holy Spirit makes His presence known in us, we can be a bit scared. It's totally natural and Heaven knows it already. Courage is the call of Gods people. The inheritance of the saints has always had the prerequisite of courage. *Have I not commanded you? Be strong and courageous. 'Do not be afraid; do not be discouraged, for the LORD your God will be with you wherever you go.'* –Joshua 1:9.

Joshua defeated 31 kings during his conquest to secure Gods promise to His people. Joshua spoke with prophetic power when he called the sun to stand still. Joshua might be well known for his conquest. But the very people who he led into promise wanted to kill him for his courage 40 years earlier.

Numbers 14:6-10 *Two of the men who had explored the land, Joshua son of Nun and Caleb son of Jephunneh, tore their clothing. 7 They said to all the people of Israel, "The land we traveled through and explored is a wonderful land! 8 And if the Lord is pleased with us, he will bring us safely into that land and give it to us. It is a rich land flowing with milk and honey. 9 Do not rebel against the Lord, and don't be afraid of the people of the land. They are only helpless prey to us! They have no protection, but the Lord is with us! Don't be afraid of them!"*

10 But the whole community began to talk about stoning Joshua and Caleb. Then the glorious presence of the Lord appeared to all the Israelites at the Tabernacle.

The people rejected faith and courage. As a result, 40 years of wondering in the dessert. God had to show up daily building faith by the provision of manna. God sustained their clothing. God caused water to come out of rocks. God protected them and provided for them for 40 years. After 40 years of supernatural provision, the next generation was ready to enter promise. Those that grumbled against Joshua and Caleb never entered the promise land. The Devil's will is to cause fear to reject faith. The Devil's will is to cause us to want to kill that which is courageous. The Devil's will is to keep you circling promise, but never conquering a thing. The Holy Spirit, the fullness of the Spirit brings courage to speak according to the Rhema word of God, thus destroying the principalities and powers of the enemy. When we embrace the fullness of the Holy Spirit, we are as Joshua and Caleb ready to conquer the promise. The Devil's will is to keep you from ever walking in promise by keeping you scared.

Americans are the most anxious people in the world. 10% of Americans have clinical anxiety. The world average is 7.3%. The United States is one of the most prosperous nations in the world, but it is also the most anxious and afraid. Americans have become increasingly fear and anxiety driven people. Each

Generation in America is reporting lower mental health statistics. According to the American Psychology Association, the Baby Boomer generation reports 70% in good mental health. Generation Z our youngest generation reports 45% in good mental health. The driving forces are stress, anxiety, and depression. The stressors on these younger generations come from several sources. One of the greatest stressors is the awareness level of brokenness in the world. The increased awareness of injustice, shootings, police brutality, and access to cyber bullying is causing a sense of powerlessness and anxiety to wash over a generation.

Numbers 13:31-33 *But the men who had gone up with him said, "We can't attack those people; they are stronger than we are." 32 And they spread among the Israelites a bad report about the land they had explored. They said, "The land we explored devours those living in it. All the people we saw there are of great size. 33 We saw the Nephilim there (the descendants of Anak come from the Nephilim). We seemed like grasshoppers in our own eyes, and we looked the same to them."*

The Devil's will is to keep you aware of and fixated on the scale of opposition so that you never take up the Spirit of God as a sword and secure a promise. The Devil is okay with you circling promise as long as you never actually secure it. The Devil's will is to make you feel small compared to him. The Holy Spirit gives you the courage to face everything standing in the way of Gods promise with courage.

Those who oppose the full operation of the Holy Spirit are many. Cries of heresy come from well-meaning and scared pastors all over the world. To embrace the full power of the Holy Spirit is to put hand to grip on the sword and take by force what God has promised. The Devil's will is to kill the voice of courage. Just as the whole community of Israelites wanted to stone Joshua and Caleb for expecting supernatural victory; stones are thrown by those who reject the full manifestation Holy Spirit, healing, prophesy, deliverance from demons, and speaking in tongues as common in the life of the believer. Have compassion on these people; they are simply scared because they brought a book to a knife fight.

I believe Jesus when He says *These signs shall follow them that believe; In my name shall they cast out Devil's; they shall speak with new tongues; they shall take up serpents; and if they drink and deadly thing, it shall not hurt them; they shall lay hands on the sick, and they shall recover.* -Mark 16:17-18. Do you believe Jesus? Is the blower on your furnace? Are you shifting the atmosphere when you walk into a situation? Are you full of courage? Are you full of the Spirit?

One of the greatest fears about taking the risk to pray for someone is this: What if God doesn't show up? Seems valid. But I assure you; this is simply stinking thinking. Those who believe must abide in Christ. He abides in them that believe. We must rephrase the question to: What if I am not abiding in Christ? If you are abiding in Christ, He abides in you by His Spirit. If He calls you to do something, He will supply His proper outcome by abiding in the your words as your words are His words. The truth about the Spirit is that you must abide Him to do anything worth doing. Abide in Jesus and crave His full residency in you. Never stop short of full submersion in the Holy Spirit. *Where the Spirit of the Lord is there is freedom.* -2 Corinthians 3:17. You can be free of fear, shame, condemnation and every device of the enemy to keep you powerless by abiding in the Spirit and the Spirit abiding in you. When the Spirit dwells in you, you become limitless as the Spirit is without limit. The Devil's will is to limit you and get you to accept every limitation. Stop being fearful that God won't show up; start being intentional about abiding in Him at every expense. The Spirit is ready to move in.

I CAN'T REMEMBER
THE LAST TIME I SHOWERED

'Food is fuel.' My mantra when I try to implement healthy goals. In honesty food isn't viewed as fuel without this reminder. Food is fun, food is satisfying, and food is a stress relief, and food represents community to me. Viewing food as fuel is far from first nature to me. If I am going to achieve my goal, I have to change the way I think. Changing the way I think is literally repentance. The Greek *metanoeo* means to change your mind. *Metanoeo* is a two-part word. The first part is propositional shift; change. The second part is thinking, frame of mind, perception and understanding. The call to repent is to change your mind, shift your perception, and reshape your understanding. Repentance is agreement with God on a level that it changes the way you think about the subject matter. The prepositional shift of mind is in the awareness of the nearness of the

Kingdom of Heaven. *'Repent for the Kingdom of Heaven is near.'* –Matthew 3:2 Agreement with God is made because of an awareness of the presence of the King and His Kingdom.

Change your mind about sin. The only way to change your mind about sin is to agree with righteousness. Righteousness is hitting the mark 'one who is as he should be.' Sin is missing the mark, 'falling short of the glory of God.' You cannot repent from Sin and remain a sinner. When you change your mind about sin, you have to agree that righteousness is Gods intention for your life. The Devil's will is to confuse repentance so that you never actually agree with righteousness.

When I view food as fuel; I think about my bodies needs when I think about food. The goal and food need to jive in harmony in order for me to reach my goals. Self-discipline is a fruit of the Holy Spirit, and is also applied to our repentance.

2 Peter 1:3-9 *His divine power has given us everything we need for a godly life through our knowledge of him who called us by his own glory and goodness. 4Through these he has given us his very great and precious promises, so that through them you may participate in the divine nature, having escaped the*

corruption in the world caused by evil desires.

₅For this very reason, make every effort to add to your faith goodness; and to goodness, knowledge; ₆and to knowledge, self-control; and to self-control, perseverance; and to perseverance, godliness; ₇and to godliness, mutual affection; and to mutual affection, love. ₈For if you possess these qualities in increasing measure, they will keep you from being ineffective and unproductive in your knowledge of our Lord Jesus Christ. ₉<u>But whoever does not have them is nearsighted and blind, forgetting that they have been cleansed from their past sins.</u>

-I can't remember the last time I showered

Confession. Sometimes I get really out of rhythm. I know life is too crazy when I can't remember the last time I showered. I typically bath 2-3 times a week; once a week or less seems to be a more natural life than my wife is willing to allow me to commit to. I become increasingly aware of my need for a shower when the deodorant gives the effect of spraying cheap cologne on a bloated pig. When the cover-up is no longer effective, it's time to clean up.

Every so often when life gets crazy, I realize I missed on my shower rhythm. Usually it's just busy-ness keeping me from a shower. Usually I am still putting confidence in my trusty deodorant routine and unaware of the reality. Again, my wife is amazing and amazingly honest with me; she makes sure I know when the cover-up deodorant doesn't work anymore. Every effort to cover up your stink will eventually fail, and you might be the last to know it. What you need is a cleansing. Repentance is like a shower. It washes all the stink away and makes you refreshing to those around you. There is very little more attractive to my wife than when I smell delicious. I never smell delicious after forgetting to shower. Repentance is agreeing that my methods of covering up the smell don't work, showering does.

How often do we trust in a single act of agreement with God, rather than a lifestyle of it? We still live in the world, this place is messy and dirty; we need to remember to bath in the waters of repentance often. It's the Devil's will to get you to trust in a single act of repentance so that you don't walk in continual agreement with God.

Acts 2:38
Repent and be baptized, every one of you, in the name of Jesus Christ for the forgiveness of your sins. And you will receive the gift of the Holy Spirit.

Repentance and baptism go hand in hand. Baptism is so many things; but for this application, lets imagine it is a bath. We change our mind about sin and agree with God, we are submerged in the waters of repentance and come out clean. Then we go into this filthy place called the world, how might we think we are going to stay clean the whole time? Can anyone honestly tell me they never relapsed and allowed sin to become part of their lives again after being cleansed of it? The fact remains, we still stain our hands with sin from time to time. Where there is the stench of sin, there is the need for cleansing repentance. I need to live a life of continual repentance, agreement with God, so that I don't live a life of continual sin.

Religious activity has a way of deodorizing us. Instead of bathing, I trust deodorant until it no longer is effective as a cover up. In the same way, many people trust religion as the cover up for their brokenness. Many churches sell their deodorant at the rate of 10% of your gross income. The Devil wants you to believe that the church and religious activity is a good enough cover up for the fact that you still stink. You'll only fool people for so long. You can *be sure your sin will find you out* –Numbers 32:23. Headlines of the moral failures of spiritual leaders all over the world are evidence to this point. Spiritual leaders are not the only ones, eventually everyone who attempts to cover their lifestyle of sin up with religion will be found out, and they will be chief hypocrites and blemishes to the reputation of the church. My goal as a spiritual leader isn't to sell the best deodorant, its to lead people to a lifestyle of repentance; agreement with God, so they can be refreshing and free. Do not trust your religious activity to be your cover up; eventually you'll just smell bad. It's the Devil's will that you trust your deodorant so much that you're the only one unaware of how much you stink. Repent, agree with God, and be cleansed for real.

Deuteronomy 6:1-9

Now this is the commandment, and these are the statutes and judgments which the Lord your God has commanded to teach you, that you may observe them in the land which you are crossing over to possess, 2 that you may fear the Lord your God, to keep all His statutes and His commandments which I command you, you and your son and your grandson, all the days of your life, and that your days may be prolonged. 3 Therefore hear, O Israel, and be careful to observe it, that it may be well with you, and that you may multiply greatly as the Lord God of your fathers has promised you—'a land flowing with milk and honey.'

4 'Hear, O Israel: The Lord our God, the Lord is one! 5 You shall love the Lord your God with all your heart, with all your soul, and with all your strength.

6 "And these words which I command you today shall be in your heart. 7 You shall teach them diligently to your children, and shall talk of them when you sit in your house, when you walk by the way, when you lie down, and when you rise up. 8

You shall bind them as a sign on your hand, and they shall be as frontlets between your eyes. 9 You shall write them on the doorposts of your house and on your gates.

The primary command is to love God with all your heart, soul, and strength. The statutes and commandments are all in obedience to one ultimate command, loving God with all that you are. *'If you love me you will keep my commandments,'* John 14:15. Loving God is the reason to follow His commands. Repentance should not be to avoid consequence. The Devil's will is to make you believe that keeping the law is to keep you from hell. God wishes for us all to be obedient out of love, not fear of judgment. Repent of this one thing right now: thinking wrong about Gods character. We love because He first loved us. It is His love that enables obedience to repentance. Repentance is a beautiful act of love, not a knee jerk reaction to the fear of hell or repercussions on earth. If you love God you will live in consistent repentance for the sake of love.

My wife and I enjoy a beautiful marriage. Every morning we say a daily vow to each other while holding each other in the middle of the kitchen. We modeled our traditional marriage vows into a daily version. Every morning I get to hear her pledge her love, faithfulness, and support. I in turn do the same for her. We start our day reminding ourselves and each other of our love, commitment, and faithfulness. This practice was not a response to any failure in our marriage. We realized after 13 years that we couldn't remember our vows. We knew we were committed to each other, but we didn't have a reminder to build us up in that commitment. The practice of our daily vow has been so beneficial in starting the day off well. We tend to be naturally resistant to these things until it's too late. We tend to assume we are committed to God, or our spouse until the hard stuff happens. When failures happen, they are crushing emergencies. In the same way, we can get into a rhythm of religious practice and volunteerism and slowly drift away from the love covenant we have with Jesus.

God instructed the Israelite community to put the command to love God with all they are, along with the commands we follow out of love all over their homes and as accessories to their daily wardrobe. The people needed constant reminders of their commitment to love God because *we all, like sheep, have gone astray, each of us has turned our own way* Isaiah 53:6a. Moses knew this too when he was delivering Gods commandments. Moses spent 40 days away from his people while God gave Moses his commandments. When Moses returned the people had made a golden calf to worship and had already declared it their God. It had been barely a month and the people already forgot everything God had done to deliver them. The people all had gone astray without the daily reminders. This is why God instructed through Moses for them to write the commands all over their homes, and even themselves. People are still people. It only takes a little while to forget the greatest of miracles God does in your midst. It only takes a little while to forget who it is we love with all of our heart, soul, and strength.

Therefore I urge you, brothers, on account of God's mercy, to offer your bodies as living sacrifices, holy and pleasing to God, which is your spiritual service of worship. $_2$Do not be conformed to this world, but be transformed by the renewing of your mind. Then you will be able to discern what is the good, pleasing, and perfect will of God.
-Romans 12:1-2

Now the Lord is the Spirit, and where the Spirit of the Lord is, there is freedom. $_{18}$And we, who with unveiled faces all reflect the glory of the Lord, are being transformed into His image with intensifying glory, which comes from the Lord, who is the Spirit.
-2 Corinthians 3:17-18

The nature of love is sacrificial. Love is not self-seeking. God has demonstrated His love towards us through mercy. The love of God led Him to hang on a bloody tree. He already offered His life as a living sacrifice. Now it's our turn to love. Notice there are two images and two processes. One in conformation to the world, the other is transformation into His image with ever increasing glory by the renewal of the mind.

Conformed: *syschematizo,* to fashion oneself according to a pattern or way of thinking and living.

Transformed: *metamorphoo,* to change into something else, to be transfigured, to take a different form.

Repentance is agreement with the Word and Spirit of God on such a deep level that it turns you into something different from what you were. What is not natural for man becomes natural for those that are transformed. What was natural sin character for man becomes unnatural for the transformed. God does not sin; it isn't in His image. Repentance doesn't mean you will try harder not to sin any more, it means you think differently about God, self, and sin so much so that sin is no longer the natural response. Repentance relies on the power of the Spirit and Word to transform our thinking so radically that we become something greater.

I am a saint saved by grace through faith. I am a new creation. My sin is separated from me as far as the east is from the west. I am not a sinner. Repentance has transformed my thinking. As a man thinks in his heart, so is he. I agree and re-agree with Gods love. I agree and re-agree to live completely sold out and in love with Jesus. That's what repentance is.

Repentance is the changing, or transformation of the mind by the Spirit of God. Every action has its initiation with a thought. Our mind controls every function of the body. If we want a transformed life, we need a transformed mind; there is no way around it.

-Remodeling a room

Repentance is like remodeling a storage room into a bathroom. We are transforming the space. Let's assume I bought a toilet and cleared enough space in the storage room to set the toilet on the ground without proper plumbing. Let's assume I declared it a bathroom because it has a toilet in it. Let's assume I used that room as a bathroom Wednesday after taco Tuesday. Has the room been transformed? The answer is yes. The room has been transformed from useful to useless. A perfectly good storage room is now the world's worst bathroom, and it smells like it too. I'd be crazy to do that. Adding something doesn't equal transformation. Adding memorized scripture to your life does not transform the mind; it's only part of the process. Transformation is not addition; it's transformation. You cannot keep the old patterns of thought, making just enough room for a few verses and expect transformation; it doesn't work that way.

Step one of renovation: See the possibility and resource it. A plan and budget must be in place before renovations begin. What's the model for repentance? The mind and image of Christ. Jesus is the only good and perfect model for transformation. We must see Him clearly before we can see the potential to become transformed into His image by the renewing of the mind. We must also calculate the cost. What will it cost to bring in plumbing, fixtures, and lighting? What will it cost me to be transformed by Christ? Once there is a clear vision and resource, begin renovation. Once you see Gods goodness, lay yourself down as a living sacrifice, it's worth it.

Step two of renovation: Clear the room, make a mess, and clean the room. The first thing we need to do is clear all of the things out of the room; they no longer belong there. Likewise, we must completely clear everything. A new mind doesn't have old baggage. Throw it all at the feet of Jesus, count it all as loss compared to knowing Him. Now make a mess of the large fixed objects. Smash them to bits. Likewise there are lies, strongholds, and footholds the enemy might have in your mind. These require force and rejection. These might be tougher to remove, but they have no place in the plan for transformation. Lastly, clean up the mess. Sometimes life gets messy when we are throwing out things that don't belong. Relationships can get messy too during this process. Be ready to clean up the mess in preparation for what God is building. He wants to build on a clean slate.

The final step of renovation: The build. Build according to the plan. Put things as they should be, (righteous is a man who is as he should be.) Let the peace of God rule. This is when you can install your toilet and call it a bathroom. You'll find when you renovate according to a well-resourced plan that things go just fine. Before long the room will be transformed into something new, with a new function and purpose.

Repentance requires continued reminders. When you go into your transformed bathroom, do not start using it as a storage room again. Resist every urge to use your bathroom as a closet ever again. Remind yourself of what the room is and forget what it was. Forget what's behind you and press on towards the goal of Christ transformation.

I want to know Christ—yes, to know the power of his resurrection and participation in his sufferings, becoming like him in his death, ₁₁and so, somehow, attaining to the resurrection from the dead.

₁₂Not that I have already obtained all this, or have already arrived at my goal, but I press on to take hold of that for which Christ Jesus took hold of me. ₁₃Brothers and sisters, I do not consider myself yet to have taken hold of it. But one thing I do: Forgetting what is behind and straining toward what is ahead, ₁₄I press on toward the goal to win the prize for which God has called me heavenward in Christ Jesus.
Philippians 3:10-14

Repentance does not equal shamefulness. Repentance results in the transformation of the mind based on love for God, His Word, and His Spirit. The Devil's will is to keep you believing repentance is just an act of will against sin instead of transformative power towards righteousness in the likeness of Jesus.

1 John 3:18-22
My little children, let us not love in word or in tongue, but in deed and in truth. ₁₉ And by this we know that we are of the truth, and shall assure our hearts before Him. ₂₀ For if our heart condemns us, God is greater than our heart, and knows all things. ₂₁ Beloved, if our heart does not condemn us, we have confidence toward God. ₂₂ And whatever we ask we receive from Him, because we keep His commandments and do those things that are pleasing in His sight.

The evidence we are of the truth; the Spirit is truth, our hearts are assured and do not condemn us. This leads to confidence towards God and the relationship to ask anything from Him and to receive it. The evidence of the relationship of love is the keeping of His commandments and doing what pleases Him. Repentance is not living in a constant state of condemnation; this limits the rest of the intended progression. The intended progression is that we no longer are limited by shame. Our minds are transformed by agreement with Gods Word and Spirit. We become empowered by freedom to ask anything in agreement with God and receive it from Him. The Devil's will is to keep us shameful, condemned, and powerless by confusing the full intention for repentance.

-Goodness and Kindness lead to repentance

Romans 2:1-5

You, therefore, have no excuse, you who pass judgment on someone else, for at whatever point you judge another, you are condemning yourself, because you who pass judgment do the same things. 2 Now we know that God's judgment against those who do such things is based on truth. 3 So when you, a mere human being, pass judgment on them and yet do the same things, do you think you will escape God's judgment? 4 Or do you show contempt for the riches of his kindness, forbearance and patience, not realizing that God's kindness is intended to lead you to repentance?
5 But because of your stubbornness and your unrepentant heart,

you are storing up wrath against yourself for the day of God's wrath, when his righteous judgment will be revealed.

Are you storing wrath up against yourself? There are two main contributors to storing up wrath: Passing judgment on others, and passing judgment on yourself. Both of these judgments show contempt for the riches of Gods kindness, forbearance, and patience. God's kindness leads to repentance. Contempt for His kindness and goodness leads to a judgmental spirit. Some versions translate 'kindness' from 'God's *Kindness* is intended to lead you to repentance' as 'goodness.' Read together we get the idea that it is His Goodness demonstrated in gentle kindness that leads us to repentance.

I struggle with the idea that repentance is simply an act of sorrow and desperation to escape the wrath of God. *The fear of the LORD is the beginning of wisdom, and knowledge of the Holy One is understanding.'* Proverbs 9:10. To be wise is not to be in constant fear of God. The beginning of wisdom is the beginning of agreement with the source of all wisdom, Jesus. Fear of His wrath is a real thing. Many people accept the substitutionary sacrifice of Jesus for themselves as a means to escape wrath. There's nothing wrong with this, we just cannot stay there. Wisdom has its beginnings in fear. Understanding, or sound judgment is found through knowing God. We have to press past the fear towards a gentle and loving King. Knowing Him deeply and intimately leads to deep and true understanding. Where does understanding come from? The Spirit transformed mind. The transformed mind, the repentant soul, might have its start with sorrow and fear; that's only the beginning, there is so much more. The Devil's will is to limit repentance to its origin in sorrow and fear so that you never discover transforming understanding through knowing God intimately.

God wants to reveal Himself as good and great to you. If we believe the lie that repentance demands a constant state of fear, we will allow fear to tell more lies. Fear tells us the lie that we have to judge others out of 'love.' Fear rooted in incomplete repentance and the under-renewed mind will send havoc into your heart and the hearts of those around you. God's goodness shown in gentle kindness leads to repentance. There might be a little fear in the beginning, but it quickly leads to a place of rest in His great love. Forgiveness has its root in power. God demonstrates the 'riches' of His kindness by through forgiveness.

Do not store up wrath for yourself by condemning yourself and those around you. Store up power through grace. Agreeing with Grace should be the thing that satisfies the fear response. Agreeing with the divine nature of God demonstrated in forgiveness, goodness, and kindness will lead to a transformed and powerful life. Repentance transforms the mind by the power of the Spirit. A transformed mind is a transformed life. Be transformed by His kindness and goodness. Repent, He is near with goodness and kindness in His hands.

AFTER THE INTERVIEW

Who said, *"Repent for the kingdom of Heaven is near"* in Matthew 3:2? Jesus? His disciples? It was a prophet on the edge of Judah near the banks of the Jordan River. He was the forerunner to Jesus. He was the voice crying out in the wilderness. John the Baptist. John had a baptism of repentance; John wanted to prepare the way for Jesus by getting people to agree with the Kingdom coming. The whole Judean countryside came out to John to be baptized in expectation of Jesus coming. I think this is beautiful. Today, so many churches still function according to the ministry of John the Baptist rather than the commission of Jesus. Well-meaning church leaders call people to repentance and baptism; but everything is still near, or coming. These churches continually prepare people for a coming, rather than bringing the Kingdom that has already come and continues to come with increase.

For unto us a child is born, unto us a son is given, and the government will be upon His shoulders. And He will be called Wonderful Counselor, Mighty God, Everlasting Father, Prince of Peace. 7 <u>Of the increase of His government and peace there will be no end</u>. He will reign on the throne of David and over his kingdom, to establish and sustain it with justice and righteousness from that time and forevermore. The zeal of the LORD of Hosts will accomplish this. –Isaiah 9:6-7

The commission is not to preach a coming Kingdom, a coming heaven, a coming judgment, a coming healing and a coming freedom. The commission is a demonstration of what has come.

Later He appeared to the eleven as they sat at the table; and He rebuked their unbelief and hardness of heart, because they did not believe those who had seen Him after He had risen. 15 And He said to them, "Go into all the world and preach the gospel to every creature. 16 He who believes and is baptized will be saved; but he who does not believe will be condemned. 17 And these signs will follow those who believe: In My name they will cast out demons; they will speak with new tongues; 18 they will take up serpents; and if they drink anything deadly, it will by no means hurt them; they will lay hands on the sick, and they will recover."

-Mark 16:14-18 (The Great Commission)

Then Jesus came to them and said, "All authority in heaven and on earth has been given to me. $_{19}$ Therefore go and make disciples of all nations, baptizing them in the name of the Father and of the Son and of the Holy Spirit, $_{20}$ and teaching them to obey everything I have commanded you. And surely I am with you always, to the very end of the age."
-Matthew 28:18-19 (The Great Commission.)

When you read both accounts of the Commission from Jesus to His people we see the whole commission. There is an evolution from the teaching and baptism with expectation of what is coming, to the making of disciples of nations, demonstration of Kingdom Authority through the casting out of demons, spiritual language, dominion over the earth, and healing. If you are anything like me, this is a little hard to digest. It's much easier to believe the Devil's lie, and agree with the Devil's will that I cannot do what God created me to do. I cannot fulfill the great commission if I do not function in the authority to demonstrate the Kingdom. The commission is a demonstration of Gods authority, not the education of mans doctrine. The commission is not just to go preach. The commission is to demonstrate the Kingdoms Authority as you make disciples. The forerunner to all the supernatural things is the

preaching. *So faith comes from hearing, and hearing through the word of Christ.* Romans 10:17. The faith that comes from hearing should lead to the faith to live as Christ lived. The Passion Translation of 1 John 4:16-17 beautifully states what it looks like to be disciples of Jesus. *We have come into an intimate experience with God's love, and we trust in the love he has for us.*
God is love! Those who are living in love are living in God, and God lives through them. 17 By living in God, love has been brought to its full expression in us so that we may fearlessly face the Day of Judgment, because all that Jesus now is, so are we in this world.

All that Jesus now is, so are we to be in this world. The commission is to bring us to such a deep love experience with Jesus that He places His seed, His signet ring, and His Spirit upon us. We conceive His Spirit. We participate in His divine nature. We look like and act like Jesus as He enables us. To be a disciple of Jesus is to yield to His authority and instruction. He wants us to function like Him, better yet, as Him in this world. I felt a surge of energy when I wrote that. God doesn't just want us to function like Him; He wants us to function as Him. His Indwelling Spirit wants to function as God functions because they are one and the same. Everything we do under the influence of the Spirit is no longer done by us, but we function as God does. He is in us, we are in Him. We do what He does, say what He says, and go where He goes because it's His life we are living in by His Spirit.

Don't get the last statement twisted; we function as God but not as a replacement or as gods. The greatest faith Jesus found on earth understood this principle. The faith of the centurion in Matthew 8:5-10

When Jesus had entered Capernaum, a centurion came to him, asking for help. 6 "Lord," he said, "my servant lies at home paralyzed, suffering terribly."

7 Jesus said to him, "Shall I come and heal him?"

8 The centurion replied, "Lord, I do not deserve to have you come under my roof. But just say the word, and my servant will be healed. 9 For I myself am a man under authority, with soldiers under me. I tell this one, 'Go,' and he goes; and that one, 'Come,' and he comes. I say to my servant, 'Do this,' and he does it."

10 When Jesus heard this, he was amazed and said to those following him, "Truly I tell you, I have not found anyone in Israel with such great faith.'

The centurion understood that anyone operating under authority operated as if they were the one who as the authority. This is the signet ring. The Holy Spirit is a seal, or signet upon our hearts. It gives us access to all authority in heaven and on earth, Jesus' authority. When we operate according to the guidance of the Holy Spirit, we are exercising authority as if we are God. The greatest faith Jesus found during His time on earth was the faith that was able to say, I function as the one whose authority I am under. If I am submitted to the authority of God, I can operate with that authority as if I were He, under His guidance and will.

When they came to the crowd, a man approached Jesus and knelt before him. 15 "Lord, have mercy on my son," he said. "He has seizures and is suffering greatly. He often falls into the fire or into the water. 16 I brought him to your disciples, but they could not heal him."

17 "You unbelieving and perverse generation," Jesus replied, "how long shall I stay with you? How long shall I put up with you? Bring the boy here to me." 18 Jesus rebuked the demon, and it came out of the boy, and he was healed at that moment.

19 Then the disciples came to Jesus in private and asked, "Why couldn't we drive it out?"

20 He replied, "Because you have so little faith. Truly I tell you, if you have faith as small as a mustard seed, you can say to this mountain, 'Move from here to there,' and it will move. Nothing will be impossible for you."
-Matthew 17:14-20

This all sounds like fairy tales and dragon smoke being blown up our behinds doesn't it? It's so easy to cast off that which we don't understand. It's so easy to measure these statements against a limited church history and decide they are not for today. But really, it's simply a lack of faith. Remember from the chapter on the truth about the Spirit I wrote: *Every attempt to explain why the Holy Spirit isn't alive and active in prophecy or healing is a demonstration of the Devil's will. The Devil's will is to make us a bunch of talking heads, using lots of wise words, but denying their power. Having a form of Godliness but denying it's power.* If you've gotten this far in the book, you should be ready to accept that smallness and misappropriation of faith is why these things have not been common. It is the Devil's will to keep the extraordinary commission from ever becoming ordinary. The Devil will manipulate scripture, history, your pride, and out right lie to keep you from having just a mustard seed of faith in the instruction for your life found in the great commission.

Teachers are listened to; Disciplers are followed. Leaving the commission to teaching and baptizing alone is not what God designed the church to be. The church is not supposed to be another educational facility with optional attendance once a week. The beauty of being a teacher is when the class is over, so is the work. Teachers are listened to. People love teachers. Teachers are very important. Teachers are

God ordained within the five offices of leadership. Teachers are not disciple makers though. Not automatically. Disciplers are followed. Their lives are watched and carefully imitated. Their words are felt and repeated. Disciple makers have no bubble privacy outside of the bathroom, bedroom, and prayer closet.

-Getting past the interview

"Here, read this book." It's a start for sure. I say it all the time myself. This is not discipleship; it's an interview.

My dad taught me a lot about interviews. He showed me how bad posture can be a good thing when done correctly in an interview. Lean forward, on the front edge of your seat. Rest your elbows on your knees if you need to. Look the part. Make good eye contact without being creepy. Listen intently as if everything they say is life changing because it could be. Respond confidently. Maintain enthusiasm, and ask the right questions. Does this sound like a good interview to you? I can say this, I have never been turned down for a job that I have interviewed for, and I've had many jobs. It works. But this doesn't just look like a good interview to me. It actually looks like what most church leadership call good membership.

Most pastors would give anything to have a room full of people who are on the edge of their seat, looking the part, listening intently as if their life depends on it, enthusiastic about where they are, and only asking the right questions at the right time. Most pastors would assume they are making disciples as they preach and pray. The fact remains, this kind of church participation is only an interview for deeper things; no pastor should ever settle for a church of perfect interviewers.

Education is key; reading books and talking about them is super important. Still not discipleship. "Here, read this book" is the second interview. It's the testing ground for compatibility and commitment. If after a week of handing a book to someone, they haven't begun to read; I know they are not committed to the kind of discipleship Jesus calls us to.

No one who puts his hand to the plow and looks back is fit for the kingdom of God. – Luke 9:62.

Jesus called his disciples in a radical way. The context of Luke 9:62 covers many very valid excuses not to drop everything and follow Jesus with complete abandonment, none of those excuses were good enough. The call to discipleship is a high calling, too high, too big to fit into any church program. It is the Devil's will to trust a program to teach us more than to be abandoned to biblical discipleship. Disciplers are followed; Jesus said, "Come with me." Discipleship is incomplete where there is no following.

I have found as a disciple maker that it's hard, painful, and inconvenient. The benefits of having a disciple do not immediately outweigh the initial investment. As I write this, my wife and I are in the process of receiving new disciples. They are moving into a tiny 500 square foot loft apartment in our church. We happen to live next door and consider this an extension of our home. They will practically live with us for a while. They are leaving the home they made for themselves, abandoning their immediate plans for buying homes and building family to focus on being discipled. My wife and I will be spending every waking moment we have with them outside of work schedules. They will eat meals at our table and even attend family functions and vacations with us if possible. Our lives will be totally uncovered before them. They will see us work through hard things and model Jesus to the best of our abilities. They will watch our lives and measure them against our instruction from the pulpit. If anything, making disciples is an inconvenient and terrifying invasion of our personal life. They will see me for who I am, and if they don't see Jesus in who I am, I am a hypocrite and failure. It's so much easier to talk the talk, than to walk the walk in front of someone all day every day. Following is the first step out of the interview process. It's scary and invasive; it's where discipleship begins.

Twice Paul said *'Imitate me as I imitate Christ'* 1 Corinthians 4:16 and 11:1. Discipleship is exactly that.

-Cultural settings and real life.

My wife likes watching football more than me, and I like watching football a lot. I had to learn quickly when we were dating that when the Green Bay Packers were on, nothing else was on. I got to see emotions I didn't know existed in the house. The rollercoaster they were on looked like the ride of your life. I had to get on that ride. I played football for a little while in my youth, I didn't know watching it was like a sport of its own. When football was on, the culture in the house shifted. There was unity and passion around the game. Everyone watched intently, made penalty calls before the refs and gloated about it. Food was often involved and there was a great sharing of both celebration and sorrow. After the game was a lingering emotional imprint, almost like the ringing of the ears. To be honest, it wasn't too different from going to church earlier that Sunday morning. I learned to share something with exuberant emotional expression in rare unity and harmony. I didn't know watching football had that kind of power. The power of football created cultural shift. The culture would slowly shift back, we would become individuals with differing taste and opinion between games; real life would settle in, and we would lose the harmonics football created for a few hours. Again, this is so similar to Sunday morning church, isn't it?

Cultural settings are beautiful. Cultural settings can bring temporary harmony to what otherwise may be a bit disjointed. But cultural settings are not the best place for discipleship – real life is. Church services create a cultural setting for harmony, sharing in celebration and sorrow. Church services create a culture of participation, teaching and learning. The church service is one of my favorite cultural settings, but I am not teaching people how to create a church setting of harmony. If the goal of discipleship is limited to the cultural setting, it never impacts real life in the way it was intended to. I have to bring people into my life in order to disciple them at a real life level. This shifts the culture of the life permanently.

-Every Creature to Nations
And He said to them, "Go into all the world and preach the gospel to every creature. –Mark 16:15
Therefore go and make disciples of all nations, baptizing them in the name of the Father and of the Son and of the Holy Spirit, 20 and teaching them to obey everything I have

commanded you. —Matthew 28:19-20

The Gospel preached to the individual, should lead to eventual real life discipleship. The Gospel is preached, and then it's modeled in real life. Notice what it says, *"Make disciples of all nations."* The power to shape a nation has always been one person at a time. The goal isn't to shape individuals, but to shape nations through the means of individual discipleship. It's exponentially powerful. One person can shape the nations through biblical discipleship. Let me tell you what doesn't shape nations: interviews, 'here, read this book,' church attendance, 2 hour visits to a cultural setting. Discipleship transforms lives faster and more effectively than any other method on earth. Discipleship in real life is the working model for the expansion of the Kingdom. Transformed people have the power to transform their people, family, and city. Transformed cities have the power to transform neighboring cities and states. Transformed regions transform nations through a working example. Transformed nations have the ability to bring the whole world to a full frontal view of Jesus Himself. Jesus is waiting eagerly for that very moment. Everything world-changing starts with just one idea, one event, one person, and one decision. Decide today to change the world by becoming a disciple, or if you've been poured into, start making disciples of Jesus Christ.

-The lonely superstar

I remember doing a series of school assemblies with a popular speaker and artist. After a marathon of pouring himself out, running on the fumes of accolades from school to school. He nearly collapsed onto a grassy hillside and let out a deep sorrowful sigh. He was tired, but not the kind of tired I assumed. He looked at me, eyes full of longing and said 'Everything I do means nothing without biblical discipleship.' Thousands of students encountered a man of God. Over a hundred people choose to put their faith in Jesus in just one day. This man longed for a disciple so much that it clouded the glory of evangelism for him. He was living in the tension of wanting a disciple to follow him everywhere he went, and a world that will settle for an assembly and a prayer. He was spending himself for the masses while longing to spend himself entirely on a few. He had become a lonely superstar longing for a disciple. It wasn't for a lack of people that admired him; it was for a lack of understanding what biblical discipleship truly entails.

I have people I admire in life. I can read their books and feel like I've had a conversation with them. But I would be crazy to say I've been discipled by them. Likewise, discipleship must be more than reading the bible and books written by people who love Jesus.

Unless I walk with Jesus, He isn't discipling me yet. Walking with Jesus is only done by the Spirit. Those who love Him walk by the Spirit. *If we live by the Spirit, let us also walk by the Spirit.* –Galatians 5:25. I need to be continually walking with Jesus, so that I can say, like Paul did, "Imitate me as I imitate Christ."

-Do as I say, not as I do
Bad parenting 101. Do as I say, not as I do. Bad Discipleship 101, Do as the Bible says, not as I do. Good parenting 101 setting an example worth following. Good Discipleship 101 Imitate Christ with confidence so you are not ashamed when others follow you.

We are to disciple nations. Ask yourself this question: "If everyone in the world responded to life the way I do, would I be happy with the world?" Is your example worth following? Are you following Christ with accuracy, authority and confidence? Discipleship becomes possible when the Holy Spirit is leading confidently and fully. If you don't feel confident in the example of Christ you've become, you need to find someone who confidently follows Jesus in real life, and follow him or her around for a while; that's called being discipled biblically.

The commission drives community. We must be the kind of people who lay down our independence for interdependence. We must stop hiding from real and real life discipleship. Sharing life in Biblical discipleship relationships is a rare and dying thing. It's the Devil's will to keep true biblical discipleship a rarity, so that nations are never truly transformed by the Gospel.

I think it's very possible that we all have the potential to change nations because Jesus dwells by His Spirit in all who believe. The obstacle we can't get over is fear of being a fraud. Those that live disingenuous faith will never live genuinely in plane view for discipleship to actually happen. Nations are not changed because people are afraid of Biblical Discipleship. That fear is called, the fear of man.

Isaiah 51:7-8 *"Hear me, you who know what is right, you people who have taken my instruction to heart: Do not fear the reproach of mere mortals or be terrified by their insults. 8 For the moth will eat them up like a garment; the worm will devour them like wool. But my righteousness will last forever, my salvation through all generations."*

The fear of what people will think, ridicule, or loss of approval is not a good thing. That fear competes with what is right... God's instruction. Remember God's instruction to preach the Gospel to all of creation, casting out demons, praying spiritual prayers, healing the sick, baptizing in the name of Jesus, and making disciples of nations. These are the instructions of the commission and the biggest hurdle is fear of man. It's the Devil's will to keep you from true discipleship by keeping you, and your pastor afraid of real discipleship. It's the Devil's will to kill biblical discipleship and replace it with simple education and cultural manipulation.

-Forgetting the flour

My daughter loves to bake. The Pumpkin bars she made me last week were top tier. I would weigh significantly more if she baked for me every day. There was a time when I had her baking every day.

She was binge watching a kids baking show for a week during summer break. Motivated to make delicious baked goods, she decided she'd bake. First up, Cinnamon rolls. Not an easy task for a beginner. Everything looked great. We were surprised and somewhat taken back by the presentation; even more taken back by the taste. I had a choice to make… like just about every parent who has had their kids creations; I could have forced it down and said it was good. That would have been a lie. The salt was burning my tongue it was so strong. When she asked if I liked it, I asked her to try it herself. She realized her mistake. Salt and Sugar are easy to mix up. She had to pay careful attention to the ingredients. Just because they look the same, doesn't make them the same.

The next time she baked, it was cookies. Easy: flour, butter, sugar, egg, vanilla, salt. For whatever reason she forgot the flour. This goop was put on a flat cookie sheet and thrown into a preheated oven. Within a few minutes we could smell the burning. Smoke filled the kitchen and we realized we hadn't changed the smoke alarm battery. I realized I couldn't let her keep making these mistakes. The solution was to make daily baking the assignment. She would bake every day until she stopped forgetting ingredients. Over the course of two weeks she learned the foundational skills and ingredients for basic baking.

Discipleship requires all the right ingredients to be fully stocked. Salt looks like Sugar in the same way Legalism can look like righteousness but leave a different taste in the mouths of those who taste it. The Holy Spirit is the foundational ingredient holding everything together. All of the right ingredients without the Holy Spirit is a mess waiting to happen. It's just as foolish to attempt to disciple without the fullness of the Spirit as it is to attempt to bake without flour. I know some expert bakers are going to say they can bake without flour, just track with me on the thought process without letting your expertise get in the way. It's the Devil's will for you to find a way around God's perfect instruction, don't do it.

This book has been prayerfully and strategically

written to this point in this progressive order:
Truth, Salvation, Righteousness, Faith, Love, Holy Spirit, Repentance, Commission; and to come, Dominion.

Truth holds everything together and sets us free. Salvation is from the Devil and deliverance to Jesus. In Christ everything can be as it should be, righteous. The righteous live by faith, and faith releases power to be righteous. Love is the motivation for every movement of our lives. Love is the motivation, evidenced by the Holy Spirits residency. The Holy Spirit is our teacher, advocate and the fullness of God in us. The Spirit teaches us and we respond with renewed minds and transformed lives. Those who have been transformed, filled with the Spirit, Motivated by pure love, moving in Faith, Convicted of Righteousness, Delivered and set free, and hold to the absolute truth; those people have every ingredient to fulfill the commission to make disciples of nations, cast out demons, heal the sick, and pray spiritual prayers. It's the Devil's will to keep all of these things out of reach, so you never make disciples and never fill and subdue the world.

BRINGING IT HOME

Why did God make us in His image? Take a few minutes to honestly pray and answer the question…

What was your answer? Many say God created us so that He could demonstrate His love for us. Some say God created us for community with Him. If God needed to create us, God isn't God. He is all-powerful and the only fully self-sustaining and sufficient one. God didn't need to create us in order to express love. God didn't need to create us out of some need for community. Every person on this earth was created in Gods image for a singular and specific purpose. Here we find, the meaning of life itself, and the function of our eternal existence as well.

Then God said, "Let us make mankind in our image, in our likeness, so that they may rule over the fish in the sea and the birds in the sky, over the livestock and all the wild animals, and over all the creatures that move along the ground."

27 So God created mankind in his own image,

   in the image of God he created them; male and female he created them.
28 God blessed them and said to them, "Be fruitful and increase in number; fill the earth and subdue it. Rule over the fish in the sea and the birds in the sky and over every living creature that moves on the ground." –Genesis 1:26-28

Did you catch that? We were made in the image of God for the sake of dominion. God's kind of dominion. Not the dominion man makes. The kind God makes.

Perfect dominion was seen in the Garden of Eden.
Mans dominion is destructive and chaotic, like that of the Devil. The Devil's will is to cause man to see 'dominion' as man creates it instead of how God established it.

Isaiah 9:6-7 *for unto us a child is born, unto us a son is given, and the government will be upon His shoulders. And He will be called Wonderful Counselor, Mighty God, Everlasting Father, Prince of Peace. 7Of the increase of His government and peace there will be no end. He will reign on the throne of David and over his kingdom, to establish and sustain it with justice and righteousness from that time and forevermore. The zeal of the LORD of Hosts will accomplish this.*

His dominion is peace. The Kingdom of God increases

where peace increases. The Kingdom of God is not like any earthly Kingdom we have ever known.

Romans 14:17 *For the kingdom of God is not a matter of eating and drinking, but of righteousness, peace, and joy in the Holy Spirit.*

1 Corinthians 4:20 *For the kingdom of God is not a matter of talk but of power.*

The dominion of the Kingdom of Heaven is not a religiously restrictive movement, nor is it a movement of Gospel declaration without demonstration. The Dominion of the Kingdom is a powerful, righteous, peaceful, and joyful Holy Spirit filled purpose. The Devil's will is to keep the Kingdom something we simply pray for and wait for; so that Power, righteousness, peace, and joy in the Holy Spirit never become the objective of living right now, today! The dominion we were created for is being held captive by the lie that we are captives of sin, rather than slaves to righteousness.

Romans 6:16-18 *Don't you know that when you offer yourselves to someone as obedient slaves, you are slaves of the one you obey— whether you are slaves to sin, which leads to death, or to obedience, which leads to righteousness? 17 But thanks be to God that, though you used to be slaves to sin, you have come to obey from your heart the pattern of teaching that has now claimed your allegiance. 18 You have been set free from sin and have become slaves to righteousness.*

Where the Kingdom of Heaven is, there is freedom from the slavery to sin. Where there is slavery to sin, there is a Kingdom conflict. Kingdom conflict leads to shame and cover-ups. *Then the eyes of both of them were opened, and they realized they were naked; so they sewed fig leaves together and made coverings for themselves.* –Genesis 3:7. The Garden of Eden was a place where there was no death, no sickness, and no shame. As man would work the garden, it would expand, eventually conquering the world. I may be wrong in the assumption that the Garden was meant to cover the whole earth. But what I do know is that the new heavens are modeled after the restoration of Eden with the tree of life restored. The new heavens and earth are going to be the righteous restoration of Gods intended purpose. He will rule supreme, and those that have been trained by God's discipline into righteousness will reign with Him over all of creation.

Hebrews 12:11 *No discipline seems enjoyable at the time, but painful. Later on, however, it yields a peaceful harvest of righteousness to those who have been trained by it.*

Remember; righteous is the one who is as he should be. We have to ask the righteous question: "How am I supposed to be?" or "Why was I created?" Nothing short of perfect dominion with Christ as eternal heir and bride is acceptable.

-The Rule of Touch

A family indulgence of ours: deep-fried Wisconsin cheese curds. I think they should be on the menu in Heaven. "Eat the ones you touch!" flies out of my mouth as my son fingers the whole basketful figuring which would be his next morsel. It's almost as if he didn't need reminding of the rule of touch; but rather, in awareness he was staking his claim. We laugh about it with our children. But what if the rule applied to more than just food. What if God were to apply the rule of touch to everything you touch. "Claim everything you touch for the Kingdom." This is a literal promise and command from God.

I will give you every place where you set your foot, as I promised Moses. –Joshua 1:3
The Promised Land isn't just somewhere you go, it's supposed to be everywhere you are! The rule of touch is in play when the Holy Spirit empowers a life that says, I *have been crucified with Christ and I no longer live, but Christ lives in me. The life I now live in the body, I live by faith in the Son of God, who loved me and gave himself for me.* Galatians 2:20.

In Isaiah 66:1 the LORD says, *"Heaven is my throne, and the Earth is my footstool."* We, are those who Christ lives through, He brings everything He treads upon into domination under His feet. Walk as Jesus walks, He will have dominion, He created you for this very purpose. Every Holy Spirit filled believer is to claim every ground they touch for the Kingdom of Heaven. It is the Devil's will to get you to call your fear humility, and to mask power with purposelessness. The Devil knows why you were created. Every step you take, every territory you claim, every place you bring the Kingdom; is a dismissal of the Devil's will, a casualty in the enemy's camp.

Start touching everything; claim it not as your own, but under the Lordship of Christ. Heaven is His throne. His Kingdom shall come to every place He is LORD. Start with your house. Declare out loud, "This is Gods House!" The power of God must be allowed to function where the Kingdom is. The Kingdom is not a matter or talk, but power. A list of restrictions does not equate to the Kingdom either, The Kingdom is righteousness, peace, and joy in the Holy Spirit. Decide to start with your home. Bring the Kingdom first at home. Do not ignore the home; if the Kingdom isn't primary in the home, you work in vanity.

Eli, the high priest that trained Samuel, was great at his job. He was diligent in the temple, and with the people. But Eli failed in the home. When God called Samuel He shared His plans for Eli: *And the Lord said to Samuel: "See,*

I am about to do something in Israel that will make the ears of everyone who hears about it tingle. ₁₂ At that time I will carry out against Eli everything I spoke against his family—from beginning to end. ₁₃ For I told him that I would judge his family forever because of the sin he knew about; <u>*his sons blasphemed God, and he failed to restrain them.*</u> *₁₄ Therefore I swore to the house of Eli, 'The guilt of Eli's house will never be atoned for by sacrifice or offering.'"* -1 Samuel 3:11-14. The Kingdom must come and remain in the home. The dominion God created you for must have origin in the home.

The home is the training ground. A safe place, full of grace and mercy. In the home, I command sickness to leave in Jesus name. Sometimes it works. Sometimes it doesn't. I praise Jesus every time anyways. In the home we worship Jesus. In the home we devote ourselves daily to Him and each other. The home is Gods home; honor to God will be shown at all expenses. Joshua 24:14-15 *Now, therefore, fear the LORD and serve Him in sincerity and truth; cast aside the gods your fathers served beyond the Euphrates and in Egypt, and serve the LORD. 15But if it is unpleasing in your sight to serve the LORD, choose for yourselves this day whom you will serve, whether the gods your fathers served beyond the Euphrates, or the gods of the Amorites in whose land you are living. As for me and my house, we will serve the LORD!"*

Every effort to claim the Kingdom outside of the home that is not yielded to Jesus will result in religion, mere talk, powerlessness and a loss of joy. If your efforts to see the Kingdom of heaven expand outside the home have resulted in these things, return to the home and re-submit it to Christ as LORD.

Seeing the Kingdom expand outside of the church service and home setting should be pure joy in the Holy Spirit. Everywhere there isn't joy, there isn't Holy Spirit. Attempting to expand the Kingdom without the present King is craziness, don't be crazy. It's the Devil's will to make you a crazy talking head in the public eye. The Holy Spirit is the power behind the gospel setting captives free, healing the sick, and demonstrating Gods goodness and greatness through grace.

-From Accusation to Declaration
The language of Heaven is distinctly different from the language of the Devil. The Devil is described as the *"accuser of the brethren"* in Revelation 12:10. This is the same boasting He makes in Daniel 7:11 the speaks *'boastful and blasphemous words.'* The Devil is also the *'Father of lies'* John 8:44.

Dominion has its beginnings in the home, but it works its way out of the home. The language we use is a good indicator as to what domain we are functioning from. John 8:42-47 is a great teacher on the correlation between language and Kingdom. *Jesus said to them, "If God were your Father, you would love me, for I have come here from*

God. I have not come on my own; God sent me. 43 Why is my language not clear to you? Because you are unable to hear what I say. 44 You belong to your father, the Devil, and you want to carry out your father's desires. He was a murderer from the beginning, not holding to the truth, for there is no truth in him. When he lies, he speaks his native language, for he is a liar and the father of lies. 45 Yet because I tell the truth, you do not believe me! 46 Can any of you prove me guilty of sin? If I am telling the truth, why don't you believe me? 47 Whoever belongs to God hears what God says. The reason you do not hear is that you do not belong to God."

The truth as God tells it is called prophecy. Those that belong to God shall prophesy His truth over people, situations, and cities. The prophetic voice is the creative evidence of Holy Spirit dwelling and working through the believer. When you face a tough situation, what is the 'truth you speak?' When people seek to destroy you, what is the 'truth you speak?' When hope seems lost, what is the 'truth you speak?' When someone is sick or hurting, what is the 'truth you speak?' When gossip comes your way, what is the 'truth you speak?' when people speak badly of you, what is the 'truth you speak?' There is no room for gossip in the Kingdom of God. If you belong to Jesus, you belong in His Kingdom. His Dominion shall be yielded to; His language shall become your language. There is no room for accusation against fellow believers in the Dominion of Heaven. The one who stands in accusation against believers is the Devil himself. If you stand in accusation, you stand with the Devil's will; after all, he is the accuser of the brethren.

In my home, there is no room for accusation. We give our kids a chance to settle matters in a godly manner first, and then we get involved if necessary. My 8-year-old son and 12-year-old daughter still have their moments, but they don't use accusative language. I have to say; they fight more maturely than most married couples I know. We train our household to be more aware of Gods destiny and purpose than the immediate offense. Consistent declaration of Gods truth will train us to think differently when we face an issue.

My kids are not the only ones who need training in Kingdom talk. I do too. My wife is a great teacher too. A few months ago I hit an emotional slump. My obligations were stacking up against unplanned events. I felt like I was responding to everything all the time. I felt the pressure of busy life like most people do. Things were not going the way I thought they ought to. While replacing my daughters tablet battery, I made an expensive mistake. My immediate response at the dinning room table in front of the whole family was to put my hands to my flushed face and let these words through my clinched teeth, "I am such an idiot!" Have you ever been there, please tell me I'm not the only one. Good thing my wife is quick to declare truth and reject lies. Her response reset the tone of my week.

"What did you just say!" She wasn't mad at me, she was

slaying the demon whispering lies in my ears. I felt quick correction in my spirit and my mind. She knows the truth about me the way God tells it and has no tolerance for lies. Repentance was not an apology; it was a declaration of truth to the whole family.

"I should not have said that, I must have believed a lie, I am not an idiot."

This is a culture in our house. We don't cuddle up with lies and pet them until they go away, they'll only come back for more attention. Swift correction of lies about identity and purpose is evidence of Kingdom dominion. We speak truth over each other. *The tongue has the power of life and death, and those who love it will eat its fruit.* –Proverbs 18:21. What we speak is what we bring to the individual and the situation.

I'm going to use a crude example for all of us to understand. Imagine you spent the whole day preparing a beautiful dinner for a guest. The guest was in charge of bringing a side dish. Your house is filled with the amazing smells, you are so excited for your guest to arrive and be slapped in the senses by saliva worthy overloads. However when your guest arrived, they brought a side of fresh doggy doo dew. What's your response? Are you going to be 'hospitable' and allow that crap in your house? Are you going to be kind and accepting and eat it when it's sliced up and put next to your culinary masterpiece? The proper response is to say, "I'm sorry but your brought something inside that belongs outside. You can come in, but you have to leave that outside, it isn't good for anyone." Does that sound judgmental or protective? Every day we are faced with these decisions. What will I bring to the table, and what's allowable at my table?

The Devil lies to us in the cleverest ways. The most believable lies are the ones that sound most true. People say, 'The Holy Spirit convicted me that I was wrong.' This is only half true. This is the kind of lie the Devil wants us to believe. Bear with me while I explain. Psalm 32:7 tells us what God is. You are my hiding place; you will protect me from trouble and surround me with songs of deliverance. God surrounds us with songs of deliverance. The declaration of God over the believer is not where you're standing; it is of where He intends to deliver you to. The song of deliverance speaks a new identity, destiny, and vicinity. Let's take this into consideration when we read John 16:7-11 But very truly I tell you, it is for your good that I am going away. Unless I go away, the Advocate will not come to you; but if I go, I will send him to you. 8 When he comes, he will prove the world to be in the wrong about sin and righteousness and judgment: 9 about sin, because people do not believe in me; 10 about righteousness, because I am going to the Father, where you can see me no longer; 11 and about judgment, because the prince of this world now stands condemned.

The role of the Holy Spirit is to convict the world of sin. Who are they that are of the world? Jesus prayed this way for those that follow Him, 'I am not asking that You take them out of the world, but that You keep them from the evil one. 16 They are not of the world, just as I am not of the world. 17 Sanctify them by the truth; Your word is truth. -John 17:15-17 Likewise we see 1 John 2:15-17 Do not love the world or anything in the world. If anyone loves the world, love for the Father is not in them. 16 For everything in the world—the lust of the flesh, the lust of the eyes, and the pride of life—comes not from the Father but from the world. 17 The world and its desires pass away, but whoever does the will of God lives forever. Those that the Holy Spirit convicts of sin are those who are of the world, so that they might no longer be of the world, lovers of the things of the world, or satisfiers of the desires of lust and pride that come from the world. The Holy Spirit convicts those that are in the world that these things are not going to end well. The Holy Spirit speaks to believers through righteousness that these things are not who we are. The Holy Spirit does convict the believer, but of what they have become through Christ. The conviction of the Holy Spirit for the believer is: "That isn't who you are, it's beneath you, and unfitting for a righteous prince." Repentance happens when believers agree with the Holy Spirit and reject the things that are unfitting out of a sense of newfound or re-discovered identity. The Devil's will is to continue to get believers to misinterpret the

Holy Spirit as if they were still sinners so that they continue to fall short.

Decide today what you are.

Are you a sinner, or the righteousness of God in Christ?

Are you captive or delivered?

Are you hurt or healed?

Are you accused, or justified?

When you live as the righteousness of God in Christ Jesus, delivered, set free, made whole, justified and covered by grace; you live in the dominion of Heaven. That dominion must be brought into the home with zero tolerance for the lies of the Devil. When your home has come into Kingdom dominion, it's time to take some ground. Carry the dominion everywhere you go, speak and act as a Kingdom bringer.

It isn't for us to take new territory, but to stake the claim. Jesus has already overcome the world; Kingdom bringers simply announce new rulership and dominion everywhere they go.

I have told you these things, so that in me you may have peace. In this world you will have trouble. But take heart! I have overcome the world. –John 16:33

Then Jesus came to them and said, "All authority in heaven and on earth has been given to Me. 19 Therefore go and make disciples of all nations, baptizing them in the name of the Father, and of the Son, and of the Holy Spirit. –Matthew 28:18-19

The truth about dominion is that everywhere you go, if you are indwelled by the Holy Spirit, you shall announce Jesus as King and LORD. Jesus already won; Jesus already has all the authority. We just get to declare what God has done and is doing. This is the voice of declaration. We must move from accusation to declaration if we ever wish to participate in the ever-increasing expansion of His peace and His dominion. You were created in the Image of God for the sake of the declaration of His dominion. His Kingdom come on earth as it is in Heaven. Declare, prophesy, heal, deliver, and speak truth as you carry the Kingdom wherever you shall go.

The Devil's will is to stop you. The Devil knows if you believe a lie, you empower the liar. It's always been the Devil's will to assume power. Destroy his weapons. Disarm him. Embarrass him with truth. Walk in righteousness, wholeness, and faith. Be empowered by the Holy Spirit as Christ lives through you. Let the goodness and Kindness of God permeate your being causing you to agree with every word He speaks. Learn the voice of the Holy Spirit as He teaches you to participate in all things for life and godliness. Speak as God speaks. Move as God moves. Love, as God is love. Disciple nations and see the Dominion expand for it is your purpose by design. It's the Devil's will, that you fall short, but God knows better – and by now so ought you. Have faith, Give hope, Be love.